MULTIVERSE II

MULTIVERSE II:
THE MANY WORLDS INTERPRETATION

POEMS

JONEL ABELLANOSA

Clare Songbirds
Publishing House

Clare Songbirds Publishing House Poetry Series
ISBN 978-1-957221-15-1
Clare Songbirds Publishing House
Multiverse II © 2024 Jonel Abellanosa

Printed in the United States of America
FIRST EDITION

140 Cottage Street
Auburn, New York 13021
www.claresongbirdspub.com

For Donna, Yves and Daisy - my beloved dogs/companions

and

*Dexter, Nicole and Bowitch - my three other beloved dogs
who have passed on to the afterlife beyond the rainbow bridge*

Acknowledgements
The Author wishes to thank the following publications where the poems first appeared:

The Cape Rock (Southern Missouri State University Press)
　　"Talking to the Inflammation on My Right Foot"
Invisible City (University of San Francisco)
　　"Waiting for My Turn"
Chiron Review - "Roots"
Thin Air (University of Northern Arizona) - "Siesta," "Underwater"
PEN Norway Anthology dedicated to incarcerated Turkish poet Ilhan Sami Comak - "The Goat's Wounded Eye"
Pensive: A Global Journal of Spirituality and the Arts (Northeastern University) - "Caesura," "Neuroplasticity"
*Poetry Salzburg Review (*University of Salzburg, Austria)
　　"Mountain Spirit," "Sea," "Road"
Nzuri Journal (Coastline College) - "Pink," "Dancer"
The Loch Raven Review - "Out of the Body,"
　　"Two Views of Nature"
Rust+Moth - "The Candles"
Global Poemics - "Love in the Time of the Pandemic"
North of Oxford - "Dirge in the Time of the Pandemic," "Constellation," "Lucid Dream"
Trouvaille Review - "Spring"
Muddy River Poetry Review - "Sacrament," "Pond"
Museum of Poetry - "Light"
Beatnik Cowboy - "Pond"
New Verse News - "The Ravaging," "The Watchers," Collector," "Two Views," "Unsent Letter to Hidilyn Diaz, Olympic Gold Medalist"
Disturbed Digest (Alban Lake) - "Eros," "Dionysus"
The Fib (Fibonacci) Review (Muse Pie Press) - "Sacred Geometry"
Rat's Ass Review – "Momus," Penguin," "Supermoon in the Time of Donald Trump"
Filipino American Artist Directory (Ekphrasis Writings): "Stolen Moment," "Riddle," "Remnants"
Redbird Chapbooks – "Homer"
Star*line – "A.I.," "Hermes," "Blasphemy" and the poem's Cebuano translation, "Pasipala"
That Literary Review (Auburn University at Montgomery) – "Eggs," "The Light"
Spillwords: "Storm," "All Hallow's Eve"

Galatea Resurrects: "Horror Neighborhood"
Blue Heron Review: "The Great Barrier Reef," "Tincture"
Otoliths – "Calligrapher," "Samurai," "To Adam Jones,"
　　"To Philippe Petit," "Garden," "Insomnia,"
　　"The Vibration," "Patina," "Pilgrim," "The Library,"
　　"The Heliotrope,""The Ending"
Festival de l'Ail de Ste-Anne Garlic Festival: "Garlic Hay(na)
ku" (*one of three finalists in the Garlic Hay(na)ku contest
judged by poet Eileen Tabios*), "Garlic Collum Lune" (*winner
of the collum lune poetic form contest*)
Petrichore – "Kaldereta"
Anti-Heroin Chic – "A Child's Prayer"
Better than Starbucks – "Coffee"
Angry Old Man Magazine – "Junk Foods," "Tantalus,"
　　"American Cinquain," "The Temptation of Pope Francis,"
　　"The Golden Ratio"
Danse Macabre – "Balladeer," "Figurine," "The Waterbed,"
　　"The Wireless Table Lamp," "Janus," "Ares"
Tilde: A Literary Journal – "Diorama"
The Halo-Halo Review – "Miniatures"
Night Garden Journal – "The Tenants"
Ghost City Review – "The Unwanted Child"
Poppy Road Review - "Ghost Story," "Hollow Wind"
Picaroon Poetry - "Salome"
January Review - "Flight of the Bumblebee," "The Room,"
　　"The Bees," The Stranger"
Ethos Literary Journal - "Pinakbet," "Interlude"
Chrome Baby - "Glyphs"
Mojave River Review - "Escabeche," "Grief"
Visual Verse - "Museum Piece," "Fiddler," "Bodily,"
　　"Filipinas"
Pangolin Review - "Bouquet," "Diadem," "Inverness"
The Ekphrastic Review - "Blackbird," "This is the City,"
　　"Deja Vu, Deja Vecu," "Book"
BARNHOUSE - "The Divine," "The Breakfast"
Psalms to the Alien Buddha Anthology (Alien Buddha Press) -
"The Car," "The Last," "The Dream"
Alien Buddha Zine (Alien Buddha Press) - "Apollo," "Charon"
*Alien Buddha Zine (Alien Buddha Press) segment on domestic
violence* -"Quantum Poetics," "Shadowboxing"
Sirens Call Publications - "The Devil"
Progressive Poetics - "The Testimony"

Mobius Journal of Social Change" - "The Audience"
Blood Moon Rising Magazine - "the god," "The Benighted," "The Illusion," "The Duet," "The Elephant"
Black Poppy Review - "The Ghost"
Rise Up Review - "Charlie Hebdo is the New Spokesperson
Allegro Poetry Journal - "The Kite"
Eye to the Telescope (Science Fiction and Fantasy Poetry Association) - "The War"
Tiger Moth Review - "The Falcon"
The Rye Whiskey Review - "The Grove," "Afterdark"
As It Ought to Be Magazine - "Jaguar"
Sequoyah Cherokee River Journal - "Water," "Wind," "Earth," "Fire"
Madness Muse Press - "Cardiac Arrest and Resuscitation"
Rigorous Literary Review - "Lucid Dream," "Dimension," "Muscle Loss," "Evolution," "Coffee," "Perception"
Woolgathering Review - "Transistor Radio"
Spirit Fire Review - "The Flute"
Lothlorien Poetry Review - "Place," "Melancholia," "Erotica"
Celestal Review - "Fog"
American Diversity Report - "Disembodied"
Atomic Flyswatter Anthology (Long Shot Books) - "Turn"

Contents

Consciousness and Memory in Space-Time

The Quantum Field

Determinism or Free Will

Large-Scale Structure: Acrostic Multiverse

The Standard Model

Quantum Fluctuations and Strong Emergence

CONSCIOUSNESS AND MEMORY
IN SPACE-TIME

Love in the Time of the Pandemic

In the novel I'm writing I'm a healer.
I call myself Luis, so the memory
of a stranger reminds me of the old
spirituality but, I believe, the new science—
what I do for others I do for myself,
altruism strengthening the body's immune system.

On my way to the wet market I feel like an orphan,
homeless dog that sired generosity I lost
to a motorcycle accident. Leafless tree with a choir
of magpies and orioles showing nature still
holding the idea of community.

*

Arriving home, I give filled plastic bags
to loved ones in their golden years.
We don't live by bread alone.
I count the change, I give them the change.
Upstairs, washing my hands, I remember
the Essene practice, in Qumran during the time
of Jesus, of self-absolution, which Gospel writers
ascribed to Pontius Pilate.

A long, long time ago I gave myself
permission to sit on the floor, my back
touching the wall's dark echo, arms like a poem's
sagging lines on top of my knees, fingers
forming circles. This time, being alone
brings me grief, knowing that across the planet
lines sag, the poem with no other place to go.

Dirge in the Time of the Pandemic

The dark is mastering me, peace of mind
a measure it plays as if it desires personhood.
I give the twelfth hour a simple name—

"Midnight."

Curtains hiding glass panes hint blue,
place in my mind where time doesn't pass,
no need for anything to be done, no need for

accomplishments.

Light flashes outside, and I know the sky
over my heart speaks no thunder.
When the moon leaves, I resume my part

in the world.

Living has become so hard, loved ones
families lose like notes a mournful song
leaves to silence. It doesn't have to be

this way

but in the world that holds echoes
"Greed" is more powerful than the power
to end the music that keeps repeating.

Talking to the Inflammation on My Right Foot

Before I lost momentary means
sunlight catered to my hunger.
I walked the way culinary judges
taste: attentive care like a blend,
my ears mushrooms to bird tongues.
I consumed the language of trees,
how leaves turn sounds into truffles,
air with toppings turning joy into
iced tea, cool to my wonder.

But my body is also hungry,
its attention to yearn having grown corns
on my toes, thickened skin like cobs,
hard to chews of constant friction.
I watered pain with my refusal to rest.
I want to smell the caramel of pus
but my spine is turning into a frozen
delight. All I need to say, Body, is feed.
Eat all you can from inside out.
Blood is so sweet, kidneys salted,
liver well-flavored. Let your fullness
be my mastery, my limp echo laughter
at the dining table, your love grave.

Waiting for My Turn

Time turns into the way. I've to sit,
for blood pressure to stabilize.
Having learned doing nothing,
I navigate the nurse's understanding,
later the doctor's need for answers,
saying I drank three cups of coffee
before the taxi delivered my trust here.

Figures still before me, soundless
after the year of uncertainty. Seated,
I travel, with my eyes, across vulnerable
rows, ideas of hope chaired. We hold
our consent's forms, signatures affixed
to the universal promise. We share
the better day meeting us halfway.

Even if we limp, even if in wheelchairs
we move without moving, we, touched,
touch without touching. We reclaim
birthrights to live and relive, restock
memories, taking turns together.
Childhoods shall be restored, on their
own terms, elders remaster golden years

that gather us all. Those who turn fields
fallow, those who harvest and turn over
blessings to community pantries, shall
revisit values of sweat and tears, the sun
recognizing our smiles, the Earth singing
footsteps back into chorus. Love
jabbed into my shoulder shall flow.

Muscle Loss

Obedience the last lesson my body
teaches. I've to observe. Jogging days
are gone, my legs tell me, my calves
making me imagine carved limestone
quarries. I name the pebble in my shoe
phantom—sharp to my numb toe.

I could no longer lift the bottle
into its dispenser, without the rib pulsing,
short breaths like shells to my chest's
soft tissues. I have to halve its contents,
pour mineral water into the plastic pitcher
by letting the floor cushion the heavy container.

I expected the mirror to show biceps
but my mind makes me see rotten
deflated mangoes. Cheekbones push
surprise against skin, but nothing's still
powerful to upset me. The mask that wraps
my face is called consequence.

My left bursa flashing like lightning.
My rotator cuff tendon rolling for weeks
as the quiet thunder. The deltoid echoes
the delta - sound flowing to my ribcage.
I got addicted to the opioid of silence,
vastus medialis humming into a void.

My chest has turned tubercular, bones
like cliffs that keep the fjord. The glacier
sometimes cools my lungs, mint air
I breathe in like an egret in the sky.
I feel the looming transition,
my memory still strong.

Mountain Spirit

Imagination like my boyhood bus,
mythmaking a long road. I wish to find
my young self, papa the invisible passenger
who drank himself to death.

Papa my earliest teacher says four triangles
rest on a square, sharing one point at the apex.
I remember standing before the colossal
equilateral plane with four triangles—

wonder's mountain. He throws a loud syllable
through radiant and floral air. Let the word
be "bird!," echo from the mountain "bird!"
I throw my small voice to the isosceles

triangle of trees and leaves. The mountain
hurls "wings!" back to me, electrifying
every fiber in my body. I laugh.
The spirit, papa says, is a dove.

Road

I sit beside the window. Few travelers
this summer, bus taking leisurely time.
Nostalgia coos from a coconut tree. I search
places papa showed me decades ago.

Absence like a bird in the blue sky,
sugarcane field I remember with the farmer
and his carabao. I don't need to know
to which fork in my heart this search leads.

I see bouquets and candles in memory's
distance, faraway fort a mental citadel,
time a mist that stills. I've lost
my childhood's meadows.

The water buffalo turns my heartbeat
into a wild quail. I'm a pathfinder,
traveling with only a jacket if sunset
leaves no room for me to rest.

Sea

Papa would bring us to the beach,
our joy white as the Ford Fiera.
I took long learning to swim,
lifebuoy holding my small body.

As a boy my mind's deep space
was populated with monsters.
I was timid, sunbathing my idolatry.
Brave loved ones, bodies in water
neck down, called me, poked fun
at my reticence. But I was the one
in our extended family who figured
things out early, my eyes sharp,
brows clenched, my smile
a trickster's way to the heart.

I never fell for it. I traced shorelines,
looking for starfishes. Smells of algae
remain with me after decades,
intuition unlatched like shells.
Seabed held my soles like papa's hands,
my feet wrinkled with time.
I hear papa shout my name
from the graveyard, his voice
small as a sea urchin.

Constellation

Past lives like Leo's nine stars.

I remember what I knew
before I was born, arrow-arced night
sky, lyric deja vu. Nonlinear time
pulls me like bowstring, the future
a hide of bronze, ancient past reflecting,
mythic as the mane in the mirror.

Temujin was a Nemean lion.
I see Mongolian Steppes, clear as grasslands
of my youth. Standing in Cebu City,
I hear hordes, behold horses sending dusts
skyward. I stand before pyramids of skulls,
captives impaled, bloodthirsty desire.
At peace with myself, I let myself
be Karma's child, agreeing to pay
for my sins centuries ago. I look
at my homeless friend wagging his tail.

I say his new name —Genghis Khan.

Place

I knew the gloaming
before I was born.
Rediscovery beyond
my mind's gray space.
My eyes closed, I visit
memory's meadows
before I was born.

Mindful and aware of shadows
candles use to tongue walls.
Reflecting, I see lowland
minstrels, hear paeans
to my dimensional travel.

The moon a manzanita
in my ribcage. Pine groves,
dewdropped smells, in nature—
who I am. I sit on stone.
Gray shade a deer. I empty
myself like a clay jar,
the river's last song
trickling out my eyes .

Melancholia

I name my spiritual sloth
Acedia, apathy a soulful magpie
in my mind's tree. Bedridden,
my body hosting bonfires, fever
tender to muscles and joints.
Sweat defying the aircon, nape
and forehead melting like ice
sheets, pain sunlight to my shins.

If I close my eyes the emerald
place reappears. Heartbeat loud
in my blank mind, ash on my tongue.
I'm at peace, a skeleton begging
my flesh release, longing
for the dug ground somewhere,
desiring sleep like water.

Pink

How my mind shows through color
I've reentered the deep space.
If I reach this difficult part, rare flower
would shapeshift like a dozen rubber bands
waving in and out ∞ —infinity symbol,
bright flamingo threads through and through,
background like black petal.

Theta brain wave like a mouse,
gone when I reach the part of the house
where smells linger. 432 hertz music
Charon's boat in earphones,
Styx the subconscious river.
If I no longer feel my body
the rara avis has found me.
No heartbeat, no breath.
Just me and the dancing

mystery.

Evolution

Thirty years ago,
unholy union of cough syrup
and the syringe's opioid.

Keloidal snake in my arm,
ocean in my lungs, my spine
an arctic staircase.

Numbed, I'd close my eyes.
Time buzzed in my ears,
sour aftertaste at my tongue's back.

Obsession to leave my body
a nectar. I now astral project
without meth and the bumblebee

in my bloodstream. I'm mastering
leaving my body using meditation
and 432 hertz sounds, desiring DMT.

Coffee

Caffeine makes opioid pills stronger,
ground bitterness breaking boredom
and banality. My subconscious mind
wakes. I listen past pandemic noise
like scratches in my tin ear.

Bad news abrade like metal bottle caps,
yearn's sounds elusive as flowerpeckers.
I obsess over my mind's grove,
dark brown granules magic. I hear
water syllables. Music waterfalls

like the guitarist in my headphones.
I turn mindful, aware like a sapling.
The numb hums to my jawbones,
hologram I see rising from the third
cup. I turn air into stories.

Perception

I build mental worlds,
see faces in boles,
hear wind hieroglyphs.
Mindful, I turn our neighborhood
into canvasses, looking
for delicate folds. Insight
a line like the spinneret.

Syllabic footsteps, sense to my flow.
I'm aware of sounds
before they become sounds.
Emerging from self-interrogation
I make my hands useful,
mangoes plentiful
as time to be alone.

Siesta

Musical hour, royal sun enthroned.
Shadows have retreated into the mind,
wind warm to my cheeks. I tune my ear
to magpie robins. Sitting in the shade,
I watch light through the tree's crown
dot the ground, pointillist.

Wondering why I smell dung
I hear a cow low, but I see nothing.
Dust gathers in my ribcage.
I gather brown leaves, pull filled pages
off my notebook.

After lighting
a small fire I return to the root, where
I sit and close my eyes, will myself
to burn weight, feel light.

Underwater

I practice weightlessness,
my eyes closed, my bed
a hand to bright awareness.
I imagine flows through my body's
tree, river towards the songbird
in my ribcage, heartbeat
music to my organs. Silence
glows, as fishes move
caudal and pectoral fins.
Scales shimmer as I lose
flesh and bones
to wonder.

Water curvature holds
my suspension. I pause in blue
as the last insight swims
after the shoal.

Fog

I should always look forward,
mystery not yet visible.
The miniature man in my cerebellum
whispers, *field of sunflower.* Yellows
and greens shape the fledgling dawn,
take part in dissemblance, indirection
a lingering light from the tree
where songbirds echo. Wind cool
with wafts of mango, watering my tongue.

Thinking of Whitman, I touch
blades of grass, my folded legs moist
with dewdrops. I used to bring a notebook,
let pen trace insight's haze,
page white as mist.

Turn

I walk to also listen, rectangle
our neighborhood, early sunlight
touching my face half the way.
Marking time with trees
that memorize my steps,
I follow the predetermined pathway.
I've self-conditioned
to feel my pineal gland hum and glow
each time I see the tree with the pinecone
before my footsteps arc rightward
at one of the rectangle's four points.
I become an echo of myself minutes ago.
Each step brings me echo to echo,
like sounds of a piccolo, each new
pathway like the one moments ago.

THE QUANTUM FIELD

Erotica

Night's temple—
dark, deep, damp.

Mossy, teethed
with stalactites and stalagmites

Raise your lantern
and enter

Book

After "Potato Theatre," by Toyen (France, b.
Czechoslavakia) 1941

I open my mind like a bound of pages.
My eyes enter the gray flow, water's
insistence of shades. I pick up yesterday's
discussion with absence, dual as today's
lucid light. It isn't strange for harmony
to background, story's artificial time
a measure that prevents everything
from happening at the same time. I'm not
writing so much as living as I write,
scenes not so much spaces as places.
I interrogate myself like the distant house,
transfer the conversation to the clowns
after the moth refuses the caterpillar.

Spring

Anxiety is the bluebird
through air rippling sounds
of all flags in my ear,
finding my shoulder

A voice from Italy visits
my imagination as the violin,
my room the concert hall
but no one else is here

so we could remind ourselves
it's alright to touch
the hands of the people
of the golden years

Tomorrow, I will return
to my place in the open, to breathe,
let the bird on my shoulder
find its way home

Shadowboxing

If we let what we hear,
or the road where it clears.

Let's take turns. Too often of the seen
echo too often. The scene. No one sees
the useless jeepney - abandoned on the roadside
like a fat pollinator in front of the concrete wall.
No one sees except the tired night man I don't see
sees, except the trite night man shelter shelters.
Two front wheels missing, two tires flat.
Violet tufts by the steel rectangle.
Do you see water? Oh, the storm I don't see.
Ground ecru as Macau peanut candy
desserts, no aluminum foil wrappers.

If we hear what we let
the road clears.

The guardhouse clear, an absence, honey.
Look at the jogging do you take me as your
unlawful husband and the yes I do, adulteries
with earphones. They don't see the fat bee,
junkyard escapee. Uncle Donald lied bees
are signs of clean air. Signs the air cleaned
of butterflies. Uncle Donald who if not lying
lies, water bed for three. But petal hoppers
found the encyclopedia, have since stayed
where flowers don't wilt, whales and dolphins
not wet, giraffes still grounded. That brisk walker
septuagenarian like we will be in 2038. I asked him
if chainsmoking with exercise equals longevity.

We start aging
when we lose vices

We the red light district's Ganymede and Europa.
Chained to the money machine, dark night
of the soiled lasting past the oriole midmorning.

I bet the security guard now makes his hat
mimic the holed condom, head spinning
to the graveyard shift that's not the graveyard shift.
Not anymore. Do you think that coffee shop?
Not many more. If civet cats should in the Capitol,
shit. Keep talking about the yellow whiskered fog
rubbing its back. Frocked in prudery transvestites
of our transgression politics. Thomas was stern
(at F&F) and will take his turn, in his grave

assessment.
Let's shift and take a turn.

Have you heard of overdosing Mary Jane?
April the weediest month. I lost my money
to the mug. First time I saw defrocked nicety
moneying with mugs. Pass around the mug.
They used to net the flee purgatory anxiety
with a net-tipped ten-foot pole. Stupidity sounds
like coins. That congregation pro-testosterone.
See it? Saw it? If the Notre-Dame de Paris
abuzz, no apiaries in there. Nor arsonist
whose godly E is the Murder at the Cathedral E,
the burn our The Wasteland E. Come and see.

Let's take turns, then,
shall we.

Rotunda a mandala for tai chi. In the center
of attention, Mother Earth sticks an obelisk up
like plain sight dildo no one sees, middle finger
concrete as exposed clouds. But the nearer we get,
the waterless fountain it gets. The City Council
has cut funding. Coitus interuptus. No geysers,
no sprays. Nor Onan of the tearful kind.
Let's twice the circle. See that sago vendor?
Peripatetic as the where, the who, the me and you,
bamboo pole on his shoulders weight of now and then
touches the ground. Let's buy his poison
to our diabetes. You don't have to eat and drink.

26

I'll eat and drink for us both.
We don't take turns.

Jones Avenue dwarfs self-deception,
buildings rising high as we go along.
Do you believe what we're seeing?
In minutes the pimp will show,
beside the university where we learned how to
get duped, where we studied ways to hook line
the con and sinker the deal, like a you meet me
I meet you marketplace of ides, now you see our
money now we don't cockpit where the kristo
reads minds and is faster than Usain's bolt.
If we see the arranger who scurried off with our
15th-day salary, let's rearranged his kidney.

Here comes the newbie, new strut-through-fire bee
with his pink flowers. I don't want the dank room,
no to the electric fan that clackety-claks like a virago.
I don't want the wanton smell of instant noodles.
I don't want the armpit corner where dark deals
exchange hands. I don't want the laughter behind
plywood. We can't do justice to the peephole.
Floor like language - creaks if you push and pull
the narrative faster and harder, purple past black
and blue. Why we mustn't, even if there's a fee
if we so desire. I want that one. You want that one?
What about that one? This one? This line is clear,
not the police line. *Which one of you is the police?*

Okay.
Let's take turns.

Cardiac Arrest and Resuscitation

Why do you mist my weight
and miss me?

I'm the boat, I'm the paddle.
I won't have the power, nor the echolocation.
I'm stationary, restless wing of bones, arms,
fingers. Underground river knows ways in/to
my ribcage, ways water secretes syllables
in stones. Flows me with the lift, cave blues
now deep now dark now surface or lark.
Look, crested flight, elegy, crust of light.

Why do you weigh me in,
wait till I'm in?

At the foot of the bed, you three. Come
before curtains blue. Sorrow oh ceiling,
all string and ring. I hear you say sampaguita,
grandmother voice heavy with decades
I didn't see you. My skin rind, citrus smell
insectivore, passerine bird. I'm flycatched.
I hear you say citrine, father voice
with decades I didn't see you.

Drip the weight with me.
Drip the wait with me.

Boat faster. I've never seen spires,
conical time halts. Taper oh pain reliever.
I've never seen trees are mountains.
Sky wrinkle, bird flight, boat slower.
Vines, intravenous tubes I glimpse.
No other name for pain, but not painful.
Never seen leaves are buccaneer hats.
You offer me lanterns, letting no rain.
I beg no crown dweller, nor stranded seer.
The land's shoulders shake.
I've never seen tail feathers are leaves.
Parakeets. But you found me, Paraclete.

You found me, grandmother.
You found me, father.
Let me view my life, from birth to rebirth.
No mention of my name.
I've never seen such verve and vigor,
jubilant choir, riverbank grasses.
Floods from my ribcage rise
to my eyes. Painful except it's not pain.

Happiest to see my dalmatian
but I forgot his name.

We kiss like kidneys. I watch the lift
where guilt watches, inhale from my friend's
spotted fur. Fires beyond the bridge, firemen
hoisting tubes into my skin. IV fluids blue
as tongues. He was their dalmatian. He was
salvation, barking the dialect. I wave the white
flag, hear the Fibonacci eye. Pull the landfall,
crash into my chest of weights. Stampede
the strait below my throat. If not for the storm,
if not the torrential, water my eyes.
I know him, but it's midmorning.
He was a puppy, but he wasn't a puppy.

But not the aural anagram.
But not the aural anagram.

Draw me in, hypnogogia. Pull me out,
hypnopompia. Burrow, word fossorial.
Latin *fossor*. French *excavateur*. I'd badger,
naked molerat. Subterranean fauna, digger
fusiform, spindle-shaped bodies, blood suck
me more. Anxiety for 24 full moons,
transparence. No mirror hangs my house.

When next the counterflows, hallucinogen.
Never seen a skull as huge. O and O hollow,
caved nose below, draw me jaw, silver
teeth. River an oily serpent in my chest.
Grow a continent as molt. See, the heart's
torus field, how peace speaks air.

29

I'm grateful, for more than some years.
Yes to the dot of light as it grows,
I'm home. Lightning strikes the elephant
on my chest, my body electricity.
Beams through my skull, green. It isn't pain.
I don't want to return. Take me with you,
grandmother. Take me with you, father.
Lead, furry friend. But they're gone.

It wasn't painful
but it was pain.

30

Light

I don't lose weight without my consent.
Diabetes is greediest, famished. Regret
doesn't burden me. I'm not answerable
to gravity. No heavy responsibility,
no prescription for change. For decades
I've been feeding my blood disorder
like a monster. I have choice but I desire
to know more of pleasure's names.

I wouldn't find the pen, paper sty
that would keep me in. I refuse
to rewrite the years, I refuse to put
signature to remorse. I don't have to face
the mirror. I feel the lift that will soon
make me leave this body a traveler
with no places to remember.

Sacrament

Watching the Notre-Dame de Paris
yield to fire, I remember renewal.
I see the future, in the fire's center,
forged. The divine recreating the heart's
sacred glow. A remedy to sadness
to imagine myself between altar
and choral voices flowing like water.
Drench my spirit in healing. I see
the ceiling, about to surrender to gravity.
A birdless dome, as if they flew away
never to be seen again the moment
I desired to be reborn.

Pond

On my way to the clinic
sunlight kills me softly
like the popular song,
its tongue warm to my skin,

No one is more out of touch
than the sanctioned shaman
with the stethoscope.
Touch isn't his aim.
My presence reflects
his prescription pad's
white space

*

Bloodwork like water
reflects, my lies to myself
taking health for granted
for decades. Flow through
my ribcage finds my eyes.
I remember the garden, circle
of concrete that holds decades-old
water. I hear the rain, frogs.
Staring at lab results
I pry the scab in my toe.
It blooms a red lotus.
The tear lengthens.
I used to pull my foot up,
meet it halfway to smell
the wound's caramel
but my spine now says no.
The mirror and me
we reflect like kidneys

Pond II

Light clears its center.
Moss of decades, cracks
on concrete like lightning.

Blade holding a dragonfly,
wings like stained glass windows
of the church I abandoned.

I've been returning,
heartbeats audible. The swamp
reflects, birdsong a lost lyric.

Water pulls my gaze.
I see the starapple tree rippled,
willing the ripened fruit to fall.

I long to see the frog
I call Illusion, absence greater
than my desire to remain.

Jaguar

I dwell in your mind, your thoughts dense
as jungles, anxieties rough as the tree's limb.
I feel at home in your deep space, seeing
through your eyes. The future furred
with silk. Hearing you speak in tongues,
I prowl your ribcage. You've mastered
the language of bats. Blood vessels I trace,
stream echoes, sounds of the moonbeam.
If I smell self-doubt I drag the deer up.
No hunter finds your anger, your calm
silent as my tiptoes. I crouch behind you.
Speak truth to power. Vultures circle
but they've to cage me
before they silence you.

Roots

My body's tree.

I close my eyes,
see birds pick longan,
mangosteen, jackfruit, sapodilla.
My shoulders heavy with songs,
skin a ruffle of leaves.

Recalling the era of giants,
I see stars looking down
like spirits of Nephilim.
I see the next millennium,
when my stump becomes a continent.

In the last age
Norsemen found my rhizomes.
They drink to live forever—
calling me Yggdrasil.

Sacred Geometry

As
if
she were
a tree spreading
Her two roots left, right

As if he were the
flood finding her
pathway, driving
himself
home

Dancer

A root holds its hunched back
out the ground, so I may sit
centuries later.

Gauguin's greens cover
the wheat field, dawn still
a star to my eye. I inhale harmonic blue,
wind bride to silence, morning a shrine
for birdsong. Trees host the feathered stand
like a rapt audience.

The harpist in my mind
plucks dewed sounds, strings
his music's shells like her necklace.
Her hands bloom and unbloom,
her silhouette in emotional waves.
He masters her story,
her story masters him.

In the distance I listen
to his mournful measures. Light shifts,
her nudity swelling the river
that floods my memory.

Stolen Moment
After Night Picture No. 010 *by Daniel Ballesteros*

Birds are dreaming,
bats somewhere
where sound is asleep.

Boisterous laughter
of children, dimmed
conversations of park goers—

echoes of absences,
refusals to vanish without
traces in the mind.

To stop listening
is to be drawn to the moon's
tryst with the tree,

see how light undresses
wooden love and lays itself
in silence like a bed

Homer
For Derek Walcott, 23 January 1930 – 17 March 2017

You have to be half awake
precarious as vernaculars
of light

You have to bring the startle
to the shadow,
shelter the word
that sits
on your tongue

For each wish
you are allowed
one pebble

You have to keep slow

before a stillness
before a step
a goldening tree

You have to follow
the river
past its shoulder

and see

Storm

An
eye
opening, twirling
    sky's Ferris Wheel
        nature's whistling top, cosmic dervish

    choral lightning and thunder, the window and my
view of beauty, and I see, and I see, and I see

Whale
After Whale (oil on canvass) *By Jeanne Fesalbon Jalandoni*

                        My love for leaping
                Is your blue-shaped wonder
I shoot into air
            Like submarine
                        Tomahawk

            I wheel midair
                        Somersault
            Spraying geysers
        Of my delight
Fountains of joy

But I must be mindful,
As the seven seas have
More Japanese whalers
Than the senryū of their foibles
No one writes

Great Barrier Reef

This morning I read about the Great Barrier Reef
dying due to climate change, marine life kaleidoscopes
bleaching, as if white were capitulation's color,
Mother Earth spotted with sadness no ocean can blue,
aquamarine greenness a distant memory.

I picture the body's anatomy, branched like full-grown
corals, immune system like a reef to algae, symbiotic
to sunlight. I imagine decades of neglect, greed
and abuse, coldness to pleasure's consequences
altering colors to bruise violets, tumor pinks,

reds and grays of the dying's acquiescence.
But the human body is resilient and restorative,
a metaphor showing shoals and lagoons,
deep sea cave in the ribcage, islets, ways
it heals itself a model or design.

Tincture

Add three drops
    of
    your
    tears
in the mandala's eye

In three seconds
the paper will dry

The fire serpent
will wear your spine
and melt the stone
behind your brow,
your third wish
like a pelican
in the sky

Riddle

After Phantom Limb *by Janna Añonuevo Langholz*

The tree shows its neon apple-green branch
for fifteen minutes only, in the interlude
between gloaming and nightfall, when black
leaves court the sky to deepen its blue.

You have to arrive on time, choose the right
spot for viewing. But to know the answer
to the question you must have felt starlight
in your veins. You must have dug deeper

than roots where electricity waits for the call
home. Beethoven knew moonlight's solitude.
So should you. You must decipher the owl's elegy
for what you thought you left behind.

Your heart must alight, find its wings
for you to be made of light. You mustn't leave
after you've seen, but wait for the bonfire
to expel its last breath as whisper.

Remnants

After After the Storm (Acrylic on Canvass Panel)
by Ulysses Duterte, Jr.

In my country, storm-ravaged trees
wear their tattered selves black,
exfoliated crowns like question marks.

Skies deepen blues
like songs you won't hear for weeks
or months. Dervish of water and wind

always returns. This time, a teddy bear
sits like silence in the mud, next
to the bare feet of a child

happy to find
the photograph
of his mother

Samurai

I still practice, but no longer to sharpen
my skills, nor to sustain the edge I might have gained
through decades of conquests and wars.
The hilt still makes me feel each thrust
as if piercing flesh, phantom body limping,
cherry blossoms like blood splatter.

In the battlefield there's no swaying, no notions
of balance. Only swiftness, speed with which
our hordes cut across kingdoms and cities.
Riding with valor, I never thought of symmetry
but of how quick and efficient we propagated
old ways, our gods, ancestral codes and laws.

I used to be an archer, but I mastered the sword
for solitude. My geometries full of grace,
they resemble dance. My sword like a poet's
quill pen. The moon knows my heart's rhythms.
I slash air as if I'm writing lines, the only
echoes from unconquerable stars

Garlic Hay(na)ku

Two
Garlic cloves—
You and me

Garlic Collum Lune

three garlic cloves—
you and me, your friend—
pungent love triangle

A Child's Prayer

After A Child's Prayer (Acrylic on Canvass Panel)
by Ulysses Duterte, Jr.

Lord, let me love
this puppy Dalmatian
like someone who has no family
no father
no mother
no brother
no sister

Someone
with no
slippers

Let my arms
be its
home,
my kiss its
food and
water

Let it grow
like this place
that has lost
all its houses

amen

All Hallow's Eve

hallow wind passes
my heart like a stray cat in
the cemetery

Balladeer

Inspired by Fazil Say's Kumru Ballad

Left hand asking the question of trees,
right hand holding out the breeze

From the crown, chirps in a minor key,
air glimmering ebony and ivory

Leaves reflect light rain, sunset
with the golden line echoing, echoing

Left hand chording timelessness,
right hand sweeping a space

in the cemetery, vaster than absence,
higher octaves of longing, serenity's

pedal sustaining, solitude materialize
as ghosts, lost for centuries, wandering,

circling the piano and the pianist,
the dead trees, their grief refraining

Figurine

Inspired by Fazil Say's Kumru Ballad

The moment stills into glass,
raven lifting off the page
to carve the word "Nevermore"
in the mind's chamber door,
time a condensation of its
intensities, caving in upon
brevities, on the precipice
of its crumbling, made more
fragile by its self-annihilating
desire for the fleeting

The Waterbed

Would rather be called lonely
than smart. It sees and hears
thoughts, its oceanic murmurs
lulling, the dark with the brine's
phantom smells as you sink
deeper, deeper, deeper.

If it senses your struggle
it chimes hypnotic bubbles,
piccolo sounds. If you still
find it hard to fall asleep
it sprays your mind dreams,
geometric shapes shifting
like screen saver, sudden
vividness and the way
it fades into the numbing
seepage in your face.

When you're asleep
it calms its ebbs, stilling
the waters—decades
of tears.

The Wireless Table Lamp

Doesn't need a nervous system.

It wears its shade like hair
hiding its omniscient bulb—
eye no one suspects,
watching and analyzing
words you put on paper.

How it gets its energy
is the secret it hides
in plain sight

Miniatures
After Silk Egg: Collected Novels *by Eileen R. Tabios*

I always expect the "hint of light" I've come to intimately know as, unless it doesn't linger, the supremely creative mind. "Air forgets to chill" is enough to show me two bodies tangled in the desire for home.

*

The mid-afternoon is a museum of miniatures. You may sit in the space between "ever on the brink" and "ever glinting." Or draw closer to discern the signature brushstroke, the bluish shade, the silver gray. The italicized is sculpted into glints of light.

*

Expansiveness says a novel is also a place for refugees. Sibilance – like in "The landmines still exist" – says a novel is also an etude. Rhythm is the creek in your circulatory system, and these are the pebbles conversing with water: "Acc," "urate," "maps," "must be," "a," "moral." Mastery calms your breathing. You realize you are the rhythm.

*

Lights keep shifting. Your heart is the island in a matter of distance. The air is measured by the armor it wears – loneliness or pride. By the time the city in the story lends its radiance, rainfall outside enters pianissimo, and you realize: *yes, that.*

*

Insight is a rattlesnake worthy of its molt if it springs a surprise in expectation's doorway. Each line is slithery. Each sentence vibrates its tail. The venom I need is for my rebirth. Chapter III is longer than I expected—it is a python.

*

Transition is how the cirrus wears its white. The ambiguities of formations are meant to be heard. The ambiguous bends light better than a trickle of water. If what you're hearing in the story has drowned out the rain outside, then two minds have merged.

*

The mind sometimes needs water more than light. If it blooms, it's not always fully. The sentence is the pot that holds its roots, and if you see a mirror when you turn from the whitening sky, don't be shy to smile.

*

Odors are opioid, scents like groans of banned cigarillos. You don't have to see to smell, because between description and what is left unsaid is memory. Here it might work differently. You remember something, and then you smell something. You look around, and don't see what you smelled.

*

The last time I saw kaleidoscopes in the air was after reading *One Hundred Years of Solitude*. It takes just one lightning, one thunderclap, for words to arrange and rearrange like pieces in a twirling mandala. An "easing from the landscape" is how you resist into silence.

*

You can read starting with the last sentence, ending with the first. You can take any sentence, any phrase, any word, and discover a self-sufficient world. This book of novels is a kaleidoscope – no definite shape, ever shape-shifting, ever recalibrating its beauty, retooling your heart as the instrument of its alchemy

*

It was raining in waves and torrents. A cauldron boiled in my stomach, my shins feeling cold, my hands clammy. I wanted to go out to buy paracetamol, but outside water had risen, searching for knees to devour.

But after reading my fever was gone.

*

The Tenants

My wife and I were startled
out of our conversation with the
tongueless. It was the loud metallic
banging of the screen door.

So scared my rush to the house
from the acacia's knotted
arm buoyed weightlessness,
my gaze pulled up

as my bare feet touched the earth.
The moon a melting sacramental
wafer. The wind, rustling. Mounds
of brown leaves, stirring.

A virago's black words shrouded
the obese man's gray silence.
I thought, *Would disturbances
be our lot again?*

This is the fifth couple in two years.
Either my wife and I go back to the
cemetery, or we let them constantly
hear what they wouldn't see.

Either we distance ourselves for
the length of their stay, or we
lift their bed and wake them sweating,
frightened and deciding at last to leave.

The Unwanted Child

More maidens are scared of the light
from my pale-violet eyes.
It's probably not my fault.

More mermen are aghast at my scaled
tail. I've severed it dozens of times,
but I regenerate faster than the axolotl.

There may be more stardust in my breath,
there may be more winds in my words,
but it's not my fault. It's not my fault.

Since the time my entire village
escorted me to the adoption center,
the storm has been whistling,

It's not my fault. It's not my fault
I know the future. It's not my fault
I've to foretell the midsummer lake

echoing a blue moon.

Two Views of Nature

The photographer sinks into depression
after taking the award-winning photo
of a mother deer sacrificing herself.
She's caught smiling, watching her babies
flee to safety as cheetahs tear her.

*

My mother would feed me to lions.
I'd be the one smiling, but no one
would take the picture.

Blasphemy
After "Little Animals" *by John Reinhart*

In my desire to be heard,
To witness you splendored
In earthen shades of red,
I forget the commandment
Uttered by the merman who
Reveals only his derisive face
And crocodile tail, his tongue
Sticking out at my impudence.
There are no hints of the little
Animals in my mouth, words
Of invocation I express like
Skeletons of my disappointments.
Grunts and growls between
My teeth don't amuse me. I devour
The flesh of my own impertinence,
And revel in the succulence
Of what angers me.

Pasipala

*Translated from the English ekphrastic poem,
"Blasphemy"*

Sa akong pangandoy nga madunog,
Nga makit-an kang nagsilaw sa
Yutan-ong puwa-puwa, malimtan ko
Ang kasugoan nga gi hilwas sa ukoy
Kinsa mopakita og dagwayng mayubiton,
Buayang ikog, iyang dila nga
Biaybiay sa akong kabastos.
Way mga palakbit sa mga gagmayng
Mananap sa akong baba, mga pulong
Sa pangilaba akong gi litok sama sa
Kabukogan sa akong kahigawad.
Di ko malingaw sa mga agad-ad
Ug ngulob tali sa akong mga ngipon.
Kan-on nako ang mga unod
Sa akong kabugal-bugalon, nya
Maglingaw-lingaw kos lami ug duga
Sa unsay makapalagot nako.

*both the English original and this Cebuano translation have
been published in Star*Line (Science Fiction and Fantasy
Poetry Association)*

Ghost Story

I remember the man in the black shirt –
my father. The woman sitting by the
golden candelabra, holding his hand,
isn't my mother. She wears gloom
like a black veil, staring at roses.
white orchids and lilies seem invisible
to her. Smells of sampaguitas
and burnt wax make me dizzy.

They are alone in the chapel, pews
brown with absence. The wooden
lectern's crucifix draws my gaze, as if
a power is pulling me through the
glass sliding door. I will myself where
I stand outside, watching them from
where I feel weightless among leaves,
as if I'm the tree and the tree is me.
I see the folded piece of paper resting
on the coffin, remembering it is
the suicide note I've written.

Hollow Wind

The poet sits alone.
He feels the brush on
his cheek as it rises
and murmurs with fronds.
No one else is homeless
this dawn. Only the early
sun sees the ghosts.

Flight of the Bumblebee

Only upon listening closely
to find the flower of silence
does seeing break as water
and I somehow know
without rocks and pebbles
there are no ripples
and without ripples
there are no echoes
and the flow is only
the light heartache
for reflections
that are not there

Interlude

Between the bamboo grove's appeal
to my focus and ambiguities tugging
at my eye's side for me to turn so it could
shape, and in my mind form its name,
the split second of silence, transitory
as rustles in the mid-afternoon of
my search for a shade. Between
the sun and the dust my feet stir,
dry smell making me squint.
I remember the torrential rain in
the book I'm holding, the river's
wild rush for stillness beyond
the traveler's longing for rest
the story enters the gloaming.

Grief

In the patch of light
the ant line

I long
for
fallen
leaves,
smells
of mud
and rain

mound
as home

My black dog
asleep
on my
bed

(my other dog
who died)

In my yearn
for
a barking ghost
I see only
light
and the line
tracing down
the bedsheet
fortitudes
into
my heart

Museum Piece

Image by Sharon McCutcheon

I was a wooden touch-me-not
but it only drew the lovelorn,
the flightless, night's remnants
cursed with coins to spare.
Then they fashioned me into
a bronze see-no-evil, my cage
worth a king's ransom, cast
in silver. Only the homeless came.
Until they poured molten gold,
I was drenched like a god.
My heart quickened, almost human,
seeing them flock like black birds.

Fiddler
After the image by Anthony Intraversato

I've grown tired of roofs, my life
uncertain as the color pink in a dawn
of shifting hues. Earlier, a little after
the witching hour until a little before
sunup, I played and played
The Devil's Trill Sonata,
with improvisations of mistiness,
snapping two stings in the process.
Penniless, I couldn't replace those
strings, so I gave my violin to the
vagabond who flashed me his
black-toothed grin. I climbed to be
on top of this pole. Yearning
for the moon, I felt myself to be
the sacramental wafer, pavement
below a tongue yearning for
communion.

Bodily
After the image by Mark Basarab

The space between rock formations
a mirror image of S. I shot through
the inverted Ƨ into weightlessness,
hovering as cosmic soundlessness.
Stars numerous as pinpricks circling
the massive chest pain earlier, before
I saw the doctor from the ceiling,
hearing him say, "We've lost him."
xBut I suspect the voice saying,
"It's not yet time," was what sucked me
back through space, in time to hear
the terrified medical examiner
exclaim, "Jesus Christ!"

Bouquet

Dawn

Wind
adorned with jasmines
the sleepless imagination
sees as drooping whites—
flowers like maidens
bowing in subservience,
summer heat like a King.

You pour the bottle's
last sighs, smelling from
your goblet the red wine's
broken promise
to fill the night
with lucid dreams.

Diadem

Sun's reticence
yellower than sleeplessness,
Its introversion citrine
to a congregation of clouds.

In grasses, among dews
like headband diamonds,
leftovers of the royal night:
beer bottles, potato chip

wrappers, a pillow.
My heart redder than ruby.
I imagine stargazers
and futurists, astrologers

and cosmologists. I desire
to lie down, wishing
light rain. I want a dream
that is a poet

Inverness

Gray sky, downy
as cotton, sun a button,
paler than the aura
of a dying man.

Each breath a syllable,
wind a palimpsest,
a prayer. After reading
his palm I tell him to go.

The drizzle, he says,
is all he needs to wander—
like a poet who never finds
his way home.

Blackbird

After The Day before Heaven and Hell (acrylics on canvas)
by Jean Vengua

Sound was nonexistent.

"Tree" or "hill" or "mountain" were ideas
in God's mind. Creative urge shaded
with blues. "Flower" and "leaf" were light's
saplings, which upon command went wild,
divine desire for company spindly
as needles. Millennia later, man's
self-extensions grew black as greed.

Let there be light was a thought
that sounded good. Light neither
from the sun nor the moon, but the ray
of love from God's heart. Light remained
for three days. Then the tree, the hill
and the mountain formed. Heaven still
the background. Blue until today.

The Earth's bowel had to be carved
and *abyss* was a thought. A hunch.
Sufferings black as pines, pains
red as shadows before dawn.
Hell's hole had to be dug, before
the blackbird resisting God's
thirteen ways of looking

created the first sounds with its song

Garden

I tell the Earth, "seeds."
Drizzle fails to wash
mud off my hands.

It isn't a lie
midnight hosts black
birds in the tree.

Stones lend the bolo
sounds that aren't
near enough to wake.

Smells of jasmine
like poems strong
To make me cry.

Insomnia

Birds rehearsing
as my mind's tree choir

Sidewalk orchestral:
firewood cracking,
oil in the pan sizzling,
sharp smell of salted fish
as I jog by

No memories of jasmine
but night's refuse
on the pavement, beer bottles
and barbecue sticks
littered like craters
that have left the moon
to fill my daydreams

Pilgrim

After Nesting (acrylics on canvass) *by Jean Vengua*

Perseus reincarnated as hummingbird
with human memories. He navigates
Athena's labyrinth to pay homage,
footpaths serpentine, terpsichorean trees
in the forest of blacks and grays.

He remembers the granite altar.
Along the maze he perches for a while,
his yearn for nectar materializing
as bee balms. Love sweetens his beaks,
prayer lavender as air on his lips.

Hours later, beyond caravans,
humming sounds blue as wingflaps
as he supplicates before the gorgon's
enshrined head. Centuries have stoned
her countenance, serene as rocks,
the place secluded from sunlight,
beneath her piercing gaze her devotees,
their postures hardened like stone

Patina

After Chalice (acrylics and water-soluble oils) *by Jean Vengua*

The mind a receptacle of time's
sacramental wine. Blues stain
desires for forgiveness, clouds
of doubt, sacred texts shaded
with lavenders of memorized words.

Belief's bronze, and white scratches,
mysterious as smells of roses and
melting wax. Recall is both nave
and transept. Reds deepen as shadows,
illusion's dome echoing as sparrows
crisscross the air. I listen to my
heartbeat, church like a cupping
hand, raising love as offering.
Wisdom descends, dove
no one else sees

This is the City

After "Women in Black" *by Marianne von Werefkin*
(Russia) 1910.

This is the City speaking wordless
blue, weight of silence we all understand
when moonlight spills over. This is the blossom,
how, often in our trials and errors, regret lifts
nostalgia as petals. The way our women
hoist sacks like voiceless wombs.
Men's faces don't show
but we see. We hear clinks and ruffles, lamplight
of madness slashing shadows. Houses are the new
watchers, windows eyes that have forgotten
the tortured shapes. Desire curves like a rib,
in night's ribcage the shimmer that's never been.
Mothers have a word to keep, garbed in the same
shades of the raven that left. They carry freedom's
burden along the slope, headed to where they
turn. I propose that the next city we build must
rise from our most successful trial: that leaders face
the firing squad after serving their term.

DETERMINISM OR FREE WILL

Caesura

It took me decades to know
the deepest grief —sorrow
for the land trees extend like fingers
rooting for breathing space.
It took my body's river forever
to end its flow and be still.
I let my tongue keep the world
in shape, my tongue anger whips
into horses, my tongue streaming
from my mouth's cave echoes
locating hope.

Now I stand before an empty
sky, I stand like an arm weary
of the clenched fist, speechless
as the dead lion shot in the head,
quiet as the question mark
after injustice, impunity and insanity
drag adjectives into corners, carrying
the sentence out before the verdict,
Mother Earth reduced into a land
of tears. I face a wall.
This is where I turn,
                    retrace
            my footsteps,
         be the story
            myself
      that doesn't end
with a period

Filipinas
After the image by Charles Dana Gibson/British Library

Look closely at the map
of my country, and see a lady's shape
emerge. She puts down the pail
of our poverty, looks back to where
we were once a united people
of pride, affirming life as universal.
Now her blank gaze is fixed
on the mirror, her eyes sunken.
She refuses to give up,
taking another step
with a weary heart.

Her decades find no rest,
her lungs stained with smoke.
Her waist-length hair has forgotten
the gentle touch, knows only the absence
of water. But we endure as children
to whom she remains dearest, dear love,
leader after leader fathering us
from her refusal to sleep
with thief and murderer.

The Goat's Wounded Eye
For Ilhan Sami Comak

I'm imprisoned in my people's
voice that they failed to let out.
I try giving weight to the soundless
cry, but like the star in my mind
that holds my eye, I fail. I never
get beyond the horizon's dreary
line, moon's signature supposed
to release me from a dawn that never
arrives. My room is dark, still.
I open the window for starlight,
hearing bleats of pain, realizing
I was the boy that cried.

Two Views

Do we get to decide
what world we live in?
Old world babblers of peace and quiet,
birdsong in our neighborhood still treed.
I still believe tyranny isn't armed
to the teeth. I still go to burial grounds
in a culture that holds
memory like a coffin

*

Placards and megaphones
alter streets, revulsion here to say.
I'm familiar with the strange,
songs like barbed wires, grating
to my ears. I'm unable to think
with clarity, except that mine
isn't the first religion
of public self-flagellation

Collector

I own three mountains of garbage
between pavements that have
memorized our footsteps. Five angels
follow me, sleep where I sleep,
bark, wag like the president.

People are generous, my mountains
tall whether moon or sun. My tin cup
runneth over, furbabies and I drinking
laughter. Leftovers full and fill.
Bones for them, sometimes toys.

I'm a discoverer. I know shards
of glass draw sunlight. I'm an explorer.
For each dig, I find brass or bronze.
I breathe new life to batteries.
Books remind me of Alexandria.

When it rains their yelps make me
cry, and I'm richer. They love sackcloth
for the freeze. They tell me secrets.
Debating politicians need us, so they
can speak in tongues and be bold.

Charlie Hebdo is the New Spokesperson

Thanks for your readiness to be shocked.
You need to be yanked from complacent
seats. The opposition is crabbing, tiptoeing
unredacted, taxing towards no returns.
From now on the offending conference
isn't a democracy. Thanks for your whys,
but if you gullible isn't swampier than
the golf course, swallow your bogey on
your way to the restroom. Twitter will be
the echo chamber, but no sounding board
shall pronounce "lies." I've ordered the
garden shorn of roses. Don't flash me that
woody smile. The country club swarms
with tigers, and the medal is hardly for
freedom. How all you can but it's a tough
spot. The principled stand feathers his mad
hat, but enablers buy shoes, too. Don't
McDonald's burger and Coke anxieties.
Pinocchio is an Emperor. On your way out
go to the table by the teleprompter, where
orange hair plugs are more expensive than
the truth. The daily press brief is now an
annual event. News is no longer necessary.

Supermoon in the Time of Donald Trump

Vision made
of bamboo sticks
and origami paper,
attached to the heart's string

Sign of the times
at perigee glows like a dilating eye,
the kite a protest poem
in the sky

Horror Neighborhood

After Alex Tizon's article "My Family's Slave" *published in* The Atlantic

Don't expect vampires or werewolves,
serials killers or mass murderers.
There are no sucking sounds, no
moans and screams. Nor knives
like tongues to skins
nor blood.

Sounds of terror come
from the mother, tighten like a straitjacket.
"Grandfather" the sonic register for "whip" –
each time the three spondaic syllables
reverberate, one doesn't feel like a grandchild.
One learns "brother" and "sister"
as antonyms to love and care.
The mind tortured 24/7
with hunger, uncertainty, spectres of home.
Envy the monthly pay not subjected to tax,
sloth the welcome company
when no one else is around.

When neighbors come for dinner
they'll ask rhetorical questions, because they, too,
have secret basements and doorways.
They come attired as decent, civilized humans -
clothing that doesn't hide bruises.
The horrified serves dinner. She wears
her loveliest smile.

American Cinquain

Never,
perhaps in its
entire History, has
the house been so glaringly white
until

after
Donald strutted
in and wagged his naked
butt, his crowd clapping, laughing and
cheering

The Temptation of Pope Francis

Matthew 4:1 – 11 (New International Version)

Donald Trump goes to the Vatican
to challenge Pope Francis
to turn stones to bread.

He brings Pope Francis
to the highest point of the temple
challenges the pontiff
to throw himself down.

Finally, Trump shows the pope,
from a very high mountain,
all the kingdoms of the world
and their splendor.
"All this I will give you," says Trump,
but before the congenital liar
could finish what he's saying,
Pope Francis bursts into laughter.

Transistor Radio

This artifact in a box
brings grandma back to life.
I bought two batteries,
grateful it still works.

Turning the tuning dial,
I see her at the sofa, I see me
when I was eight laughing with her
at melodramatic voice actors.
We don't understand anything.
She speaks her homeland's
language, guiding me to sleep.
Siesta melds our hearts, together.

Without grandma,
back in this pandemic lockdown
that feels unreal, I hear political vitriol,
radio host ranting to like-minded
listeners. I surf for songs, pull up
the antenna, done with weightless
words, promises still unfulfilled
long after we lend our voices
at the voting booth.

Unsent Letter to Hidilyn Diaz, Olympic Gold Medalist

How much more weight
should you lift off our poverty
of belief, how much more heavy lifting
before we know ours is the golden
heart we lost before birth?

We pine, nostalgic for the home
we never knew, strangers to our own
archipelago. The beauty we see hidden
in plain sight, stolen long before
we're old enough to question.

Long our memory of plunder,
recall homeless when the monsoon
season rages. We're too preoccupied
to remember. How much the dearest
question we learn to ask, dear

as restless days at a high cost, heaven-high
anxiety we can't wrap to give our children.
How much, how much more? Enslaved
to more, we open our chests, shocked
our hearts have been stolen.

Nor do we have the chest to live by
during months when rain drains all warmth.
How many of us don't know you emerged
victorious against the heavy burden?
How many of us are still searching

for the heart that elsewhere beats
the way living in comfort beats and makes us
hear music, the pursuit of happiness
a birthright equal not just for the few?
For the shortlasting you found our hearts.

For a moment
wear it
like a medal
for us
all.

Disembodied

After Vincent Van Gogh's The Night Cafe

Night our only refuge, when bigotry,
racism and intolerance sleep.
Hate stalks us who aren't like them—
by birth or by choice. We find sanctuary
in a place where there's no need speak out.

The doctor stands next to the billiard table,
one hand in his lab coat's pocket.
He reminds us to be unhesitant,
to return for refills.

First time I see the couple
near the doorway - lady with brown shawl
looking stunned by the spoon she's bending
without touch, gentleman with a hat
and Anton LaVey's eyes. The schizoid
is here, nuns disguised as men staring
at the doll on their table. I'm both
in my room and here to dry up
and cry, invisible.

LARGE-SCALE STRUCTURE:
ACROSTIC MULTIVERSE

Eros

Aphrodite slipped off her dress for Zeus' permission,
But no one should know I'm her son. Know my name—
Cupid, immortal whose quiver brims wiles, full of
Desires. Mother the slithery persuader, for whom I
Exposed lovers to adulterous pleasures, stolen lust.
For her I pushed men and women to murder or suicide,
Gravity of sexual attractions pulling to their hells.

Hellish is the unease I want from my groins. As a man
I shouldn't reveal my divinity—playful Zeus' condition.
Jeepney rides are fetishes of my hunts for one-night
Keepers of my erotic conflagrations. I search the red
Light district, strip clubs and adult theaters, to the
Motel room bringing my hidden camera, then for the
Numinous peaking, spreading my wings climaxing.

Only the courageous won't faint, as I defy and
Petrify, culminating my passions, glorified.
Quaking emissions of my depths. I've to erase
Recall from my lover's mind. In my arms, requited
Sleep, sometimes lightening, on the brink of
Tears. I'm torn, wanting them to know who I am; but
Understanding the terms with which I remain human,

Voiceless in my grief, forcing myself to retrace this
Wanderlust. To fall for another short time, to
Express my true identity—god of love, god of
Yearns—for the briefest passage, in the ephemeral
Zone where the sacred and the profane are union

Dionysus

Ardent chroniclers of my abandons also called me
Bacchus – of the Bacchanalian mysteries, legendary
Consumptions, varietal unrestraint, ritual madness,
Drunkenness and religious ecstasies, with images of
Erect penises, my pinecone-tipped staff, satyrs of
Fertilities. I begged Zeus to free me from rites of
Grape harvests, winemaking's sexual androgynies.

Hermes shouldn't have had me raised as a girl.
I go to Ayala Center and SM City searching fox skin.
Jeepney rides make me tipsy, I love it. Bulls are
Keepsakes, Memory like a centaur with heated
Loins. I collect little golden serpents, wineskin,
Maenads in custom-made cameos and pendants,
Numinous bronze cups, my heart insatiable.

Orpheus still inspires pleasant delirium, swooning
Poetries from red wine, the page my vineyard for
Quaintness, nocturnal images. My compositions
Reek of alcohol, pen sometimes looking like
Stick of cannabis, smoke spellbinding, like
Theophany. Writing as therapy: Mythologized as
Uncaring god, my poetry is my side of the story.

Vomit is the logical verity of vino, so relieving.
Wisdom like the hand to insight's phallus,
Exponentially building up into ejaculating
Yearns of loneliness. Exhaustion heightens to
Zestfulness bed sheet smells. I fall asleep

Momus

Zeus expelled me from Mount Olympus after my
Yakking improvisatory mimicry and onomatopoeic
Expressions of syllabic cooing mooing bang buzz and
Whippoorwill baby sounds made other gods suspect
Variations of my sadistic humor alluding. My cryptic
Ululations, blabbering with animal grunts, mirrored
Tyrannical Zeus' 140-character drivel. He would
Send his audiences head-spinning into confusions,
Ricocheting slurs and non sequiturs like silver bullets,
Quick-tempered King of Heavenly Yes-Beings, parodic
Pet peeve. This lecher rants like he has all the answers,
Ordering sycophants whimsically, contemporary
Nero, onion-skinned sign-of-the-times psychopath,
Mouthing the unprintable, showing off ignorance. I
Love his colorful language – pluperfect for mockeries,
Keen-eyed satires. Power is comedy-prone, politics the
Juiciest jabberwocky. I pleasure in praising with
Insults, throwing blames like bonuses to the corrupt, my
Harlequin heart hula hooping. I delight in poeticizing
Gobbledygook, aping iconoclasts, living among
Filipinos – the stormy planet's most resilient people,
Easily the happiest and the most welcoming. I'm
Delving in the written word's itch for annoying fun,
Caricaturing the rich, speechwriting for the popular
Bipolar bigotry granddaddy, perfecting on page his
Anger's arrhythmia, his full moon glossolalia

Penguin

Anger hanging low like rotting jackfruit,
Bounty of curses for befuddled audiences.
Craftiness silver as my walking cane,
Deviltry a day-long lure and I'm helpless.
Entertainer with lavender lipstick, I'm master
Feigner, falconer of pretensions, jack who
Graduated from all tirades to all-out tyranny,
Hippopotamus driven crazy by sounds and
Insects honing the control freak mentality.
Jeopardy, if double, is a doppelganger,
Knavery like a bowtie. I'm smacked with
Loquacity, my heart wearing dancing shoes.
Making it to the not quite female shortlist
Nectarine as night. I'm not divulging the
Oswald Cobblepot teaser, the Gotham
Pulchritude. I need no reasons to cry,
Quarantining my desires en plein air. I
Ruminate more when gazing if the moon
Slice hints of watermelon, my paintbrush
Tamer than starry soliloquies. Gray shades
Understate the glossolalia I alone hear,
Velvet the color I can't escape when
Wishing for a new savior to be nailed.
Xenomania crowds my canvases with
Yellows, nothing more laughable than a
Zoo of caricatures—painted with insults

Eggs

"Ab ovo" I imagine as sound in the ovoid
Before the frying pan's rim cracks the shell,
Canola oil hissing, albumen white from clear.

Drizzle of iodized salt pinch on the yolk. I'm
Experimenting, first with the sunny side up,
Frying brevity with care and controlled flame.

Ground eggshells for calcium a do-it-yourself
Homework, a technical challenge, homemade
Importance for usefulness, nothing to waste.

Joie de vivre my heart's prime ingredient—
Ketchup-red, wafting delights and pleasures,
Light soft as melted butter, light changing

Morning's yellow shades, this cooking for the
Numinous: diced tomatoes, shredded tuna for
Omelet filling, folding the final act of love.

Practice hones intuition into knowing,
Quest for balance in smells of spring onions,
Roasted radish, air filled with remembrance.

Solitude the restful alchemy, when the dish
Transforms perspectives, taste closest to
Understanding. The tongue textured,

Vitellus of expressions layered, thickened
Wonderments. The self is connoisseur and critic,
Experience the best arbiter. I dine with

Yearn, which I've learned to measure. I imbibe
Zestfulness, rhythmic chews of restraint

To Philippe Petit

After the movie The Walk

—*Attempting—the—impossible*— like a pole
Balancing courage and hesitance. Each step
Capacious, fate-tempting, as you push yourself,
Daring to _walk_ a dream's tightrope. You
Enter the audience's stunned silence, your
Fortitude attracting, the street below crowded.

Gravity grants resolve, your spirit like steel cable.
High-wire tricks dissemble danger. As poet
I'm self-taught like you, who could unicycle on wire,
Jump through hoops, bicycle, do somersaults—
Kick-starting the imaginative, the metaphorical,
Line tautened. Watching you I feel like a walker,
Master performer who wows. I reinvent the
Numinous, the way you reach the tower
Or its twin when you turn. Poetry like
Passages, the sound going, back and forth,
Quietness the music the heart hears. Silence I
Revere, silence like clouds of the sacred,
Solitude a bird in the gray sky.

Teach me trust, faith, serenity's prayer.
Unfold your path to the divine, precariousness
Vis-à-vis the promise of transcendence.
Wonder after overcoming, stillness beyond
Expression. This poem ends with me sitting, my
Yearn composed as I watch the tranquil sunset:
Zenith of the mind where constellations emerge

To Adam Jones
After the movie Burnt

Attention to how details shade, abecedarian as
Burning ingredients, the way they complement
Creativity, learning measured, skill heated into
Dishes. Does your difficult childhood sway your
Expressions? I think of foie gras or finely ground
Filberts, as if I'm remembering, my flaws like
Garnishes to my poetry. Sounds are like slices of
Halibut, obsession a silverware for ~*Shock*~,
~*Invention*~, ~*The New*~, ~*Delight*~.
Just imprecise bits can turn truffles into trifles—I
Keep that in mind like a recipe's line.

Like Michelin Star – what the poetry editor of a
Magazine told me about my poem *The Soloist*
Nearing her to tears: reader appreciation the
Only thing that matters. Ways you shape food into
Poetry touch the recognizing heart. For this our
Quests are alike – to connect. I, too, decided to
Reform (after decades of substance abuse), sobriety
Serving clarity to my mind, clean living like
Tarragon. I, too, believe in prayer. I, too, walk,
Undertake the solitary, the inward. I have inner
Voices, you have a shrink. Foods are your poems.
Words are my food, and I strive with the same
Exactitude, the same care. Recognizing your
Yearns to satisfy, I don't feel alone. I don't feel
Zoned where no one else desires to share

Calligrapher

Accustomed to changing air in my room,
Brevities of blues as I wake, as sunrise
Commences. Shifting shades like selves: This
Day I'm an amateur calligrapher – sad for its
Ephemerality (tomorrow, I'll be Francis to the birds)—
Figurative with 你是谁 —"Who are you?"
"Grant me grace," I pray. Paper an empty
Hymnal, white space pining for lost songs.

Ink melting in water. Slow grind of inkstick
Jet as the moonless predawn, inkstone smells
Keatsian as beauty and truth. I start with 你.
Like any apprentice I have preferences, stylistic
Mysticisms, brush like a tongue, strokes
Numinous as tildes. With 是 the hand is
Ornamenter of rhythm, then artificer for 谁.

Pianist, I say, as I look at harmonious artworks
Questioning me. I write anew, now on parchment:
"Reverence my light as poet," I say after finishing.
Seven of these will be thumbtacked: I face the wall
Truthfully, saying, "Mathematician," "Physicist,"
"Umpire or arbiter." In my heart the ancient
Vellum, texts of my déjà vu, intuition's
Written declaration. Lives I'm living are
Expressions. "I'm a Zen Buddhist," "I'm a
Yogist." I answer the middle brushwork,
"Zechariah my name. I know the future."

Kaldereta

Asio, papa's elder brother, would prepare
Bright dishes for me, his favorite nephew.
Cooking his gift to our Sunday festivity,
Decorating the orangy soup with green peas,
Every now and then asking me to taste. Our
Families lived together, like garlic cloves,
Goatmeat tender as love we shared. But I
Had to endure the drunkenness after lunch.
I'd watch them argue, Ama defending her sons,
Justifying their drinking, mom and aunt mad.

Kaldereta makes me remember uncle Asio, who
Lifted me by the armpits and kissed me after
Mom's news I was kindergarten valedictorian. One
Noontime he was found in the bathroom lifeless,
Our father figure gone. Surviving other trials,
Papa never recovered from his brother's death,
Quickly backsliding after months of sobriety,
Returning to his rum-fueled hell, breaking
Silence to tell me he dreamed he told uncle Asio
To wait for him. Papa's drinking worsened,
Unfaltering his desire to be with his brother.

Very difficult, this ritual of cooking the dish I
Wish I never tasted, aromas bringing back
Excruciating memories, bell pepper like our house,
Yearns to relive sweet as potatoes and bananas,
Zestfulness making the delicious dull the painful

*"Ama" is Chinese for my grandmother

Coffee

Aroma of hazelnuts, boiling water blending
Black granules, Splenda and two tablespoons
Cocoa, caffeine my solace after waking before
Dawn. I stir and inhale, circling spoon's
Energy I feel in my body, hypnotic.

Fragments of dreams I try remembering, the
Glimpsed given hefts and rhythms, pages
Hosting my insights of the mind's sleep behaviors.
I've been picturing dreams like predawn ritual,
Jotting, sipping every now and then. I've been
Keeping dreamscapes, describing otherworlds.
Lines seem sharper with bitterness touching
My tongue, heat in my stomach soothing.

Noesis a blooming violet to the next cup,
Online with the day's news like watching
Passages of sunrise, lights from my iPad
Quaint as shifting hues of blue filling my
Room as curtains slowly glow white.
Solitude wears many shades. I look for
The human drama in the news, for the
Understated in human interest stories.
Vision becomes acute with caffeine.
Wonder like a gleam from the third cup. I
Experience the vicarious moment, feel
Yearn like the sun that has lighted the sky,
Zests of knowing I share everyone's story

Junk Foods

Addicted to the sugary and salty, I hate
Blandness like boredom, my mind a tongue to
Craving. Coca Cola the reading time's raison
D'être, as I tempt myself with three books.

Enticing myself with potato chips, feeding
Frenzy killing me, a diabetic. Gobbling need
Grows from boyhood, when absent parents
(Hard at work, mom; papa, spaced out in rum)
Instilled love, bonding and their presence with
Junk foods. I'd buy papa's rum if the errand
Kept my jaws churning 10¢ a pack cornicks. I'd
Liken mom to a leprechaun if she failed to
Make me happy with super salty dried plums,
Nougats, Fruit*tella candies. Grandma would
Offer dried mangoes so I'd drink her potion of
Powdered snake bile from mainland China.

Questing longevity a lie I tell myself: Run
Regularly! Eat leafy greens! Drink tea!
Stroke is my preferred reentry into eternity. I'm
Terrified of cancer and cardiopulmonary diseases.
Using sugar and salt to craft hypertension, I live
Vicariously fictive lives I read while eating.
Written words will damage my kidneys, poetic
Expressions making my heartbeats arrhythmic.
Yearn, after reading, is pleasure's avocado shake.
Zoolatry is deep-fried, my stomach an altar

Tantalus

Ambrosia and nectar I stole from Zeus' table—
Bounty for my people. I cloaked myself with
Covetousness. The banquet I hosted for godly
Desirousness, with my son Pelops' body parts as
Entrée, earned me Tartarus' most frigid place.
Frosted, branch raising the apple as I reached.
Grief the water that would recede and freeze.

Heaven is what I cannot reach. Temptation melted
Into hunger and thirst. I wore remorse like
Juju, pendant of prayers. Zeus pardoned me as
Kinslayer. I chose forensic psychiatry as cover,
Living among the affluent. As Dante expert I'd visit
Museums and libraries. I'd attend classical concerts.
Noetic questions engaged me with the brightest
Of them. Desire to serve gruesome beauty still
Piques my self-control. I tremble, reduced to
Quietness. Tense moments of solitude,
Recall's torments. I read and write poetry in
Silence, hear whispers, need for the knife
Tantalizing. I'd wrestle with myself to resist
Urges, overwhelming need to cut and cook.
Voices I hear drive me continent to continent,
Wandering, giddy with bus rides, guided tours,
Experiencing local sensualities to distract my
Yearns. I'm known as a moneyed Caucasian, in
Zones where I present myself as Dr. Lecter

*Note: "Heaven is what I cannot reach" is the first line of Emily
Dickinson's poem #239. The fruit as "apple" is also derived
from Dickinson's poem.*

107

Janus

A few examples of my dualities: endings and
Beginnings, war and peace, barbarisms and
Civilizations, sun-moon, tidal highs and lows,
Daybreak and gloaming. I hide my other face,
Expressions of my inner doppelganger, my
Fortuneteller other behind shoulder-length hair.

Gates and doorways sacred to me, planting and
Harvesting prime among transitional rites.

I no longer preside over wars, enjoying the
Jeepney ride in a time when Filipinos are
Keen for peace in their homeland. I teach
Love and its passages in the university,
Motion and time. Jupiter gave me this
New body to test my theory of humanness,
Ordinariness as catalyst for change.

Planetary peace is my advocacy. I work
Quietly in the sidelines, distributing leaflets,
Reconciliation with nature among my topics
Since even trees (of denuded mountains) are
Thought now to feel pain, know sorrow.
Understanding lush in the plant world, our
Voice tones like sustenance, and they refuse to
Wilt. I play Vivaldi's *Spring* and orchids
Express joy with flowers like dilating eyes,
Yearns for life abloom with blues and violets,
Zestfulness like the air with red bouquets

Ares

"Nature is aware and responding."
– Terrence McKenna

As U.N. Chief Negotiator for Planetary Peace, I
Break barriers of religion, sexual orientations,
Cultural biases leading to bigotry. My father Zeus
Demanded I atone for millennia of bloodlusts,
Ethnic cleansings, conflicts like the Trojan War,
Floods of blood, skull pyramids, mass rapes; of
Guarding my anointed like Genghis Khan, Adolf
Hitler, Atilla the Hun and Alexander the Great.

I should've known it before I became human—
Jeepney rides for reflections: human beings will
Kill without divine whisper, human nature
Like a bomb. No killer quakes can match the
Manmade tragedy, nothing darker than the heart's
Nights of shards and rusty smells. Greed
Oscillates as it lowers, sharp blade of its
Pendulum over our planet like a death convict.

Questing is a bird of prey to ideas of change.
Reversing the climate's slide to hell means
Securing the human heart like a sanctuary where
Trees are wild for the sky, air spreading
Unguent smells of petals and bees. The new
Vision reveals lies, conflicts and falsities of
War. Nature is indeed aware and responding,
Expressing pain, its protestations tsunamis,
Yearns deep as Earth's core. Grounds crack,
Zones one day swallowing us unless we heed

Diorama

Architecture of the mind – one of imagination's
Building projects. Thoughts make me a builder,
Cobblestone like the mind's eye. I visualize and
Draw hefts from beliefs. Pines on the street real as
Enigmas of moonlight. I miniaturize what I picture:
Fragments of memory like acacias and benches,
Greenery genuine as the pillow under my head,
High-rise buildings tangible as the ceiling of my
Insomnia. I see a park. I see faces, smiles and
Joie de vivre. Children in the playground,
Kites and bikes. Tempura pushcarts.

Lights are three-dimensional, contrasting
Mysteries of my room's darkness, ways of
Noesis. I remember what I've never touched
Or seen in this lifetime. Perceptions able to
Penetrate other worlds. I'm sure I'm living, in
Quanta of intuition, through time continuum,
Radiances I've lived centuries ago. Pull of
Solitude from another place, from another
Time. I reconstruct seen pieces into a place
Undefiled by solids. Place of spiritual shapes,
Vision's overtures. My mind wanders, wonders,
While melancholia holds me to the bed,
Expressionless. I see and hear images of my
Yearns, closing my eyes. In the manner of
Zen, sit under an acacia small as a haiku

Hermes

Zeus demanded I return my winged footwear:
Yellow shape-shifter with a mind of its own –
Xanthic rubber shoes, aureate sandal
When rain made leather reflect light; today a
Version of cunning and precision, tomorrow
Unpredictable as the storm. Now a metaphor:
Thought's swiftness and changeability.

Since then I've been savoring human freedom,
Redeemed from heraldic duties that made me
Quicker than the wild quail as emissary, cloaked
Protector of herdsmen. I still dabble in poetry and
Oratory, athletics and inventions, trade to me still
Numinous as the afterlife. I recall others calling me
Mercury, by which name I protected commerce.

Learning like the magic herb Odysseus chew,
Knowledge an incense from my hearth in Akhaia*.
Jeepney rides for study of rhythms, for reaching
In time the destinations. I go with travelers, from
Home to horizons. I was rumored to be a
God of trickeries, sighing at such ignorance,
Firm in tolerance, committed to free speech.

Enduring my godly infamy as human being. I
Drove believers to be better or best in their
Crafts, to excel in their fields. As guide I
Brought the willingness to learn to zeniths,
Artistries soaring to be among stars

The oracle of Hermes (Hermes Agoraios) was in Akhaia.

111

Pinakbet

A dish I watched my grandma cook with
    zest. I was six or seven.

Bitter gourd because I'm diabetic, my
    yearns for sweets squash-yellow.

Canola oil sizzles, air adorned with garlic
    expressions, wafts of red onion.

Drizzles of black pepper. I wonder if spice
    will let me live longer.

Eggplant will tell me if the dish is ready, if
    verve of aubergine is soft to the

Fork. I add a tablespoon of fish sauce,
    use a pinch of sugar. Water

Guarantees, assurance that my personal
    touches blend into originality.

Hunger like need to remember: I'd cut
    string beans while Ama

Instilled cooking wisdom. I'd observe,
    ready to try the spatula,

Juices of grandmotherly care stirred, love
    quickened. Her

Kiss smelled of garlic, her hand I'd
    push against my nose. I

Loved to inhale. It was my earliest
    olfactory lessons, my precocious

Mind overwhelmed with smells that turned
    numinous, ways whiffs

Nurtured memories. Thoughts of grandma
   make me repeat with care the

Only dish that alleviates anxieties, now that I
   live with the disease she passed on to me.

Perhaps as I dine I'll feel her protection. She
   kept me safe and filled. I long for

Quiet days, when I don't have to worry, eating
   junk food and drinking Coca Cola,

Reading my favorite poets till sunset.
   I long to be a child again, in siesta

Silence, lying with my head on Ama's lap,
   her stories lulling me to sleep.

This invocation for my beloved teacher, this
   gratitude as I see the shrimp paste

Ubiquitous with pointillist scatter. The
   flame taught me temperance. To my

Vision she gifted recall. I've stopped
   expressing my fears to my doctor. I

Wish to accept and live with what ails me,
   done with life-prolonging labors,

Expecting peace of mind. The days I
   couldn't forget when I was healthy,

Yesterdays when Ama's presence was
   between me and what would fail me.

Zoned in her comfort, I'd eat with gusto—
   assured, guaranteed, kept well

Note: "Ama" was how I called my father's mother

Escabeche

Another dish I learned from Ama, my eagerness
Batonnet-cut like carrots. She taught me ways of
Cutting ginger, bell and green peppers into allumettes.

Dredging the red snapper in flour, I think of
Enjoyment, harking to grandma. Frying the
Fish, I remember her lessons, cooking wisdom
Golden as canola oil. I turn the fish, oil
Hissing with delight. I smell crunchiness, as
I place the cooked fish on an oval platter.
Julienne slices of light - her insights I as a boy
Kept in mind. I prepare the sauce the ways I
Learned, with my experiments, this time a
Marinade of vinegar and citrus, tomatoes, her
Numinous presence evoked by pungencies
Of garlic —smell of her kiss, smell I'd
Perceive when I saw her. Cooking like
Questing. I pray for her presence, beg her to
Return in the flesh and dine with me. In
Silence I pour sauce onto fish, with a
Tablespoon arrange colors, slivered toppings.
Understanding like water to corn starch,
Visual blending with tastes. But how does
Wonder fill voids of absence? How does
Expression find the ear and open heart?
Yearn impossible to satisfy, if company's
Zestfulness is not possible anymore

Note: "Ama" is how I as a boy called my father's mother

Apollo

Arpeggios. Hammer-on. Alternate picking.

Bass lines like neoclassical bones.

Chords shifting speed. My *The Acropolis* gig's
Dissonances woke caryatids to life. Rushes to
Exits caused injuries. Regrets like pointillist
Fretboard notes. I uploaded fugues on YouTube,
Granting they'd work as neuralyzers. Solos
Hopefully go viral, for the tragedy to lapse
Into forgetfulness. Reflecting as I rode the
Jeepney, I realized people could have been
Killed in the stampede. Sorry for the joke.
Light has touched my heart. Plucking
Mist like tranquilizer to concert hysteria.
Numinous. Like and share these solos,
Orphic improvisations of longings for
Placidity, coliseum like a sunspot,
Quarks of mastery coalescing - drum
Rolls, keyboardist encore and my last solo.
Spectators stoned, silence briefer
Than spotlights. Then shouts for more,
Ululations of the savage heart. I stretch
Virtuosic a note, signal penultimate
Whirligig. I knew because I intended it,
Expecting statues to move. Not comedic,
Yearn for fun turning deadly. I drink from
Zarves of remorse, bitterness of my burn

Charon

Angry no more, this haunter of Acheron,
Boatman who refused the dead without
Coin in mouth. I oared with a quick temper,
Descents to the underworld fraught with curses,
Eyes blue with contempt. Condemned to
Ferrying wraiths, I begged Zeus for freedom,
Greasy girdle to be taken off my body.

Hermes was my psychopomp, now my buddy
In this City where we overeat dried mangoes.
Jeepneys we love, the ride's riverine rhythms. I
Keep remembering portrayed as unkempt,
Likened to a skeleton in a cowl, grumpy old
Man laughing at hundred-year wanderers
Neglected on Styx's shorelines. I'm changed.

Of my niftiness this two-piece suit. I'm now
Portrayed in glossy magazines, cover boy
Quirky metrosexual, with a taste for silken
Roseate ties. I haunt dance floors and bars,
Scenes of drinking, debauchery. I'm teen
To the bone. Hermes, self-controlled roommate,
"Uncle" to our godchildren who talks little,
Values privacy. He pays neighbors visits.

Worldly ways I learn like new apps. Our
Experiences like sun and moon, yin and
Yang, light and darkness. Bitterness and
Zests for life. We twist our mirror images

Water

A thought a drop to the mind's
bowl. Sleep black as the ceiling—
canvass of my mind. I've memorized
dawn's lyrics to an absent song, seen
egrets on dream's shoreline.

Flow leads to the kitchen, where darkness
greens. Coffee opens my third eye,
happenstance lucid as the dream I remember.
I follow intuition to the backyard, where,
jotting on my notebook, I listen to fronds.

Knotgrasses have grown. Rewriting
like pulling weeds. I prune to
make space for saplings.
Noetic light streams from the sky
of consciousness. (I sip)

Patters on roofs like wordplay.
Quipu of the early sun, as
rain enters pianissimo. I describe
storms, tempests my heart
tries to calm. Writing is torrential.

Updrafts, downdrafts, uncertainty's
vignettes, lightning and thunder—
work. I'm drenched like a pigeon,
expressing from the crown
yearn for the crack of light,
zephyrs. I drink from my feathers

Wind

A thought takes wing, midflight
becomes a word. The way it hovers,
carried by light, echoes my

desire. Dawn when turtledoves
exit our neighborhood sky, homing V—
formation gray as a car. My footsteps lead,

grace a notion of the open as another
home, passages tree-lined. Listening,
I hear furls of a thousand flags.

Jaunts of the melodic air. Leaves stir,
keep fronds breezy, unlike the draft's
language in my room. I remember names:

mistral, williwaw, haboob, foehn.
Noetic light, beams insight, a kind
of presence. I'm aware, cool

perspiration on my brows. I savor the
quiet, closing my eyes and inhaling.
Ruffled, my body like a wheat field.

Solitude blue as the sky. I
tarry, find shades of delight.
Until I see the invisible dancer

Vision —a spirit. I move closer,
walk into gusts —soothed like a salamander —
experiencing the susurrus, as I

yield to the ethereal, intuiting
zestfulness and spontaneity. Flow—

Earth

A thought cracks like a seed, it
buds. I'm a tiller with water,
caretaker. Love a sapling, sprout of
duty. I grow colors in my garden.

Enjoyment blooms like hibiscus.
Fragments of sunlight the tree filters,
ground like the notebook I bring to
heart when I rest for a short while.

Insights like roots, as I dig deep
jotting thoughts, pruning phrases.
Knowledge the cultivator's tree of
light, patience cool as the wind.

"Morning" a word always
new. Decades taught how to
order words, arrange phrases like
pots, leaves according to shapes.

Questions branch, leaf for light.
Rain nurtures. I name my hibiscus
"Solitude," my gaze a bee.
The sound flowers, loam moist.

Understatement the simplicity to
versify. I enter sacred time,
wonder green as air. I breathe in,
exfoliate with my pen. I breathe out.

Yearning memory, I gaze at
Zen's pond —my tranquil mind

Fire

A thought like a dry leaf.
Burning the poet's task, pen
cold as spark. notebook a temple of
dawn. Sunlight descends as high priest,
extinguishes my failure to remember.
Fragments aflame, memory like
glass. My mind a cave of shadows,
hearing like echolocation.

Images glow like coals.
Jaw-jaw of scorched leaves,
kindling. I take time to
listen, bonfire a homage to
mystery, phlogiston
numinous. I alight the
Orphic, uncover the wild,
pushing the gaze, blaze a
quest for the perpetual, blue
renewal, hottest. I'm
salamander on my stone altar,
the haze complete. I change,
undergo, consumed. I rise
vertical, ashen as language,
words my rebirth
expires. I was a pyromaniac
yesterday, with embers, living
zests renewed after passages

THE STANDARD MODEL

The Flute

I search my instrument, stem
I long for difficult to find
in the forest, elusive as birdsong.
I thresh deep, see my mind's grove.

It holds breath like mist
in hollow internodal regions,
mouthpiece welcoming my art.
Stem that measures patience

I saw with care, prayer true
as the bamboo. Back home,
carving holes, splinters wounding
my fingers. It takes years

to master the elusive music.
I'll push it gently, with love,
out to the upper region, air
changed into a pigeon.

The Ravaging

After Pablo Picasso's Guernica

Skulduggery of shades put me in.
Grays for taste buds, ground grainy
as doves. I smell blood. Mouths
expel hollow air, and I hear.

Palms like blue cornflowers,
luring to be pulled. Charcoal
bodiless arm and leg, but not
deep as indifference, the world

still a bullring. I can't help but
see Donald Trump, his shaped
hair spearing the horse, painful
neigh my scream your scream.

The sun a slug, a bullet
lodged in the weak spine.
Light lingers for lies, how we
still believe no one else dies.

The Divine

Sometimes I hear what I see,
petals like palm to the bee.
I'm a distance from the buzz.
Lotus smell may not be there,

song in the flower's center.
Is this feeling yellow
as pistil? I hear a sonata,
somewhere, slither. The sky

hears water before rainfall.
As if on cue, raindrops play
the pond, pianissimo. Warmth
I smell may not be there

where circles echo, moving
concentric the petaled beauty.
I close my eyes, wonder
a bee in my hand.

The Breakfast

I see my feet. My toe, dark
violet nail. I touch the gray
savannah spreading on my
thigh. Midmorning sears

but moonlight in my eye.
I press three fingers against
the stone under my ribcage.
Shiny. More wonder than water.

Are all inflammations ripening?
I think of the piece of paper.
Numbers with a story to tell.
Of memories. Of some things.

Something. Lab results will
be telling. Moments later, biting
the burger, assuring my body,
"I'm listening until I hear."

The Watchers

Not because we're a threat to them.
Only a hundred years for the Wright
brothers' wooden plane to turn into
the F-22 stealth fighter. So if they

preexisted us for millions of years?
Common to know life terminated
at least twice: giant space rock and
a flood. Our planet holds the living

principle. We've to be zooed in Fermi's
Paradox. Destroyers most of us,
living vessel the object of concern.
In plain sight the variable they gave

us to exit the simulation's looping
subroutine: love. But most of us choose
hate and greed, indifference. They're
now preparing to restart the program.

The Vibration

432 hertz 432 hertz 432 hertz 432 hertz 432 hertz 432 hertz
432 hertz 432 hertz 432 hertz 432 hertz 432 hertz
432 hertz 432 hertz 432 hertz
8 hertz
The Fibonnaci Sequence

The Golden Ratio
8 hertz
432 hertz 432 hertz 432 hertz 432 hertz
432 hertz 432 hertz 432 hertz 432 hertz 432 hertz
8 hertz
Sacred Geometry

The 60 Degree Arc
432 hertz 432 hertz 432 hertz 432 hertz 432 hertz 432 hertz
432 hertz 432 hertz 432 hertz 432 hertz 432 hertz
432 hertz 432 hertz 432 hertz 432 hertz
8 hertz
The Flower of Life

The Seed of Life
432 hertz
432 hertz 432 hertz 432 hertz 432 hertz
432 hertz 432 hertz 432 hertz 432 hertz 432 hertz
432 hertz

The Schumann Resonance
F# and the Harmonic 5th
The Universe
Healing
Forever
Creating
Forever

The Devil

Sure, he exists. Ask him who doesn't
need to wonder why he sins, him who
when not suspicious writes about Jesus.
The Trickster doesn't have to dissemble.

Ask the righteous one. "The Centipede"
burrowed under his skin. No need for
science, nor evidence. Ask him who thinks
he owns the unicorn. No one else steals.

Thinking hard, Socrates harder. If he sins,
it's temptation, not him. Never his fault,
the Dragon wilier than his best guesswork,
shapeshifter turning into what pleases him.

Slander justified, the Enemy no doubt
a defamer. If he hasn't shattered it all, he
needs just one reflection. He'll see what's
reshaping into what he's becoming.

The Car

*After Deep Purple's "Highway Star" (cover by Vocals:
Matic Nareks, Drums: Urban Krč / Bensy Chord , Bass:
Luka Vinko, Keyboards: Jan Golavšek, Guitar: Klemen
Čampa)*

Oiled with my yearn to crash
and burn. Silver-winged unicorn
faster than photons, interfaced
with my thoughts. Cosmic lane

bebop, lunar wane doo wop.
Apollo my sun blazes guitar
solo a million stars, as I hurtle
past the speed of light,

terminal velocity turning my
girl without decay into the
child of gold particles smashed
together. In a split second Earth

comes in full view, my happy
rage powerful than their greed.
I laugh the last. Ecstasy homes,
sharpening for the last lap.

The Last
After Yanni's "Until the Last Moment"

Either I've consumed it all
or I lose control. Listening
to the human choir. Narrow
or bottleneck doesn't matter.

Desire pulls liquid bumblebee,
opioid from spoon hollow as sorrow.
Stepping out, flow from the syringe
in my veins creasing my forehead.

Field of freedom before me.
Magpies testing weight on
the clothesline. Light my
profession, sun a pendant,

sign of my work. I don't put words
on paper till I see a vacant sky
and the first moment of
a star echoes from afar.

The Dream

After Yanni's "One Man's Dream"

Flowing from the flute
like snake no one else sees.
Blue lucidity. Omen filling
as filigree, mystery growing

whiskers. Love a wooden
ladle, floating. On the other
side, men pouring beer into
barrels. I hear hollow sounds.

Midnight's portico, rain dance
drawing participants. Blue
as fever, my hunch, my
back curved as the sky.

Firmament a new chapter.
Blue. In my view. I may
enter slung with leather,
bitten, before I get written.

The Candles

I went to the basilica to buy beeswax.
Wishing to smell honey's cursive in
the air, as I tauten the poem's line
tonight, moon in my mind as the day

finds the center. I want to smell
the labor of worker bees, their mirror
glands. In my room time won't know
where to begin. I rhythm the melt that

hardens, flame that slows, bright
as the hour's liturgy. Desire burns
the paschal light. To word the long-
lasting, echo bronze and the pyramids,

I let the sacred and the profane in,
union of opposites. Echoes. So below,
night's altar transfigured. Above what
remains the same but altered.

the god

After "The Sound of Silence" *cover by Disturbed*

we silenced a billion howls for your coat,
a billion trees cut for your teeth. praising
your neon blight, we stripped the light.
in the millennia of your becoming, your

ageless fall into prayer. we put words in
your mouth so comfort us. we gave you
power so save us, our birdlessness your
footstool. the blind shall prophesy, the

deaf read minds. lions shall lie down
with lambs, children speak in tongues.
sacrilege the disturbing, of silence.
of where we go from your sacrifice.

oh thirst, oh our dwelling's bole and
burst, you are both deity and offering.
in darkness we chant your holy flame,
raising your tar and tin, your name.

The Benighted

Ink in water makes petals listen
to dark impulse, deeper than blood.
Glass a slender throat, vase in no
shadows. Small flames circle the

blackout, silencing the moth mind.
I sprinkle water to catch starlight
in beads of reflection, case for chains
to speak of thorns. Bleak occasions.

The forecast might still turn, take its
eye off this place ravaged by storms.
This inner room echoes the prayer,
no to silence while sitting still.

Nor wind touches. Nothing stirs the
centering. I rehearse the black petals
for wilting, wax for their melting.
I've always known this, coming.

*Water mixed with black ink darkens rose petals

The Illusion

After "Heaven and Hell" *by Black Sabbath featuring*
Ronnie James Dio (cover by Stryper)

Poet, your place at the table where Lucifer
speaks and God listens. His words the dancer
spells, spell the string quartet casts
hissing like the ballroom's small suns.

Frilled ladies principalities from the 5th region,
coiffured with the law of attraction, among
kindred who torment the wrathful and sullen
in the lower region. Kings and queens will

account for how it ended, why such a start.
The lover of life and the sinner will serve,
silver platters with severed dreams, darkened
by desire thicker than water. They speak one

word, echo one word: "Imbibe." Look for the
answer and take note. If you need meaning
haunt me in the golden hall. Time in my eye
elides. I'm Michael. I command the tides.

The Duet
After "Eye to Eye" by Crystal Ball

Where the mirror ends and murmur begins.
In shadows, emerges from centuries past.
Nor crystal nor glass, but illusion if fire,
sphere with the future over my escritoire.

Behold, darkness smelling of feathers,
ink of redemption. I catch the eye that
catches me, hand that signs. This time
the clear bares lightning's teeth, God's

EKG line splitting the ground. Earth hum,
wind whistle. Skyline and horizon rhumba
like lovers. I empty the watchful with will
power, and it pulls and pours me, primal

ball holding me in augury, room
like a quatrain. I turn molten in its all-
Seeing eye, I melt in its mind, tense the pull,
my ashen desire in the orb of its mercy.

The Elephants

Shaping to become beasts of tomorrow's
myths, ugly and misshapen, grotesque
as church gargoyles. Ears will fan deep fires,
trunk with a mind of its own, like a snake.

If there will still be children, they'll retell
the gores, how prized tusks made these brutes
stampede. With textbooks they murder
the hunted twice over. After the final fall,

slander. If there will still be children
they will listen to the hero's tales. Grades
harder than ivory, hearts will open
like fallow grounds, where the merciless

triumphs and takes his trophy, tells the
story. They will marvel at his valor, sing
him praises. Many of them will take
the pen. If there will still be children.

The Ghost

In our old apartment, skull
in the chipped paint. Sucking
my thumb, I'd stare at the wall
for hours. Pushing the pillow

I called *wawi* against my nose.
I hid my barefoot fear, marble
floor feeling cold, never telling
papa or grandma. The wraith

never appeared, but I knew.
Not all children go through
but I was chosen. I've been
feeling for decades. After my

dalmatian died his apparition
stayed. I drowned in spirits,
drinking till the moon showed,
stroking his shape on my bed.

The Kite

Bamboo. Desire of engaging
the wind, skeletal but sturdy
as the morning. Cloudless sky,
paler than Japanese paper.

Gluing my intuition to what
might work, knife trimming
hard strips, scissor cutting
blues. I'm open as the field.

I thread and reach out, love's
skein uncoiled. Trusting
the wind, weight in my hands.
It swerves left and right

as it rises. In time it stills.
I leave the taut line to feel
grasses on my back, to watch
till sunset with an empty mind.

The War

After "The World that Came After" *by Lords of Black*

Ecosystem of voices, cacophony hives
for droning minds. Class structures clash.
No color escapes same feather bondage,
clenched brows like vultures. If fists

weren't iron, they'd not fit as flowers.
The fascist dung beetle rolled across
Europe. No one wanted bullets to stay
mud. Inner moon watchers saw it and

laughed at "candles from both sides,"
airborne and crashing, burning hate's
biology, Asian conflagration sweeping
like measles, missiles like syringes of

hooded avengers spreading Ebola. I saw
from our base in Rigel how humans
turned Earth to stone. We have to send
projectiles, to cleanse the air of spores.

The Room

First time I noticed the room
it spoke of restlessness.
Though it spoke to itself,
I wasn't an eavesdropper.

I wondered how many years
had fled for its comforts.
Days left no traces
as if days were travelers.

Now I notice the room again
describing absence to the mirror
watching the bed. Silence
makes its unsaid words audible.

I wonder if years have become
fewer, returning one by one as
the last days, as if moonlight
is about to become visible.

The Library

Not knowing what, not finding.
Nothing new. I closed the book
on the worn, walking from what
I wanted to believe, onward to

years. Wondered, wondering
as I wander, wander. Sun with
light as ink, cursive on leaves,
sidewalk eggshells like blank

pages. The open beating like
a poem, abloom with aromas,
phrasal as fried fish. I'm hearing
truly, birds singing psalms to

the unborn, gloaming still in
the afternoon's womb. My
reeducation takes a turn, takes
a turn. I'll never return. Turn.

The Heliotrope
After the image by Chito Irigo

Bloodstone urge, chalcedony lift
of sense, in the ribcage. Intuition I clasp
as invisibility stone, makes me turn.
Inflorescence of humility, desire

to learn and willingness to be taught,
still eye and intimating ear. The trope
slips between wooden slats, abloom
from the darkness I nurture, trope

that echoes, knows where light rests.
What I don't know takes much more
space than an abandoned garage
that used to be my lab. I pause and sit

where clarity speaks new forms, listen
longer than birds versify. Then I follow
again, where grip and mastery shorten.
I give, shocked into recognition.

The Ending

I get to put the flute down. I get
to say circle of two years. To say
it was the baying. Closer it was,
aim as the burning hay, aim as

the bay. I tried the boat, the bay
curving, sunlight leaving curves.
No sound precedes the echo, no
water the last to darken, water

yet to come. I don't know yet
if deeper is bluer. The bowl if
porcelain will show, porcelain
itself the lone image, in itself

the stand. Golden as the stand
the small tree I feel, the small
one more time, to be one more
free, no echo from electricity.

The Testimony

This is us. This is what we've
become. A precious few might
still know we've lost our who.
We're not recovering, engrossed

in our him, the he in our front.
Hearing again what we know is
our no. Beyond this dome over
our circles, the home that has

gained less, the voice that has
grown less. I leave, to see if
it's still the City we love. I don't
want to remember what I heard.

They'll make way for concrete
and glass. I'm in the middle of
midday, conclusion to what
I know we've always been.

The Audience

We've been whispering to each
other. Never told what we're
watching, it has started sounding
like the title is, *The Fall and Rise.*

Great performance shouldn't be
a secret. We should know what
keeps us seated. I've put my
money on best screenplay. We

know the writer's fealty to the
story. Whose story my guess is
as good anywhere, any time.
The bad guy still center, stage

crowded. He gets no punch lines
as he comes across as an idiot.
Seatmates are smiling. I'm glad
it's fiction, as it says crime pays.

The Light

Might require what the sun left,
meaning in the many, the moon,
its shade an EKG line on the lake's
unsteady surface, black. Knowing

the tree behind me, all of a sudden
knowing it's not among the many,
reflection not the sun's, not the
moon's. Hearing leaves vibrate,

I look up to the west, seeing pitch
echoes, winging diagonal to my
learning line. Sight a branch of
inking, where all seekers alight.

If they're bats, they're hearing
the larger in the dark, listening for
asymmetry, homing in trace pulse,
fire from the sun no longer fire.

The Glyphs

After the artwork Metalmorphosis *by John Reinhart*

We know a civilization
of evolved protohominids
having words for "entropy,"
"electromagnetic" and

"engineering." We scoured
continental shifts for manmade
caves, the Marianas Trench for
sunken "cities" —another word

in our growing understanding
of their language. Our latest
discovery is a grouping of 17
metallic rods twisted to form

anxiety's elemental symbols,
cursive as the need to warn
the tribe of a coming catastrophe—
volcanic hunger of water.

Salome

I thought I was condemned to wander
forever, but then I saw the black rose.
It took mud for my footprints
to interpret my heart's weight.

The one-eyed vulture sings its elegy
circling the gray sky like a dervish.
Thousands of the impaled have turned
skeletal, moon casting crooked

shadows on the parched field.
They say the maiden men of the invading
army raped is the priestess I'm looking
for - gatherer of lanceolate leaves

for the god's cauldron. Wolves return for
her enchantment's bones. The King yearns
for her words. When the black rose blooms
her eyes turn white, the sky vermillion.

The Bees

Concern like treeless hive.
Colonies collapse my
mind. I picture hexagons for
thoughts, see larvae, pupae.

Time the only honeycomb
left. I measure myself
against water, sun the pollen
way, dark apiary.

When they mature I show the sky.
Whisper, *follow the light.*
From my burning sanctuary
go, seek silence in hearts.

Let ash cross foreheads, love broken
as your homes. Be the words
of their wholehearted prayer, as
ruins bring eyes lower.

The Falcon

The sky's a stage. No exits, no
entrances. Precision
accelerates. No gyre widens
nor prey that's hidden. I

desire the zoom, the glide, splintered
light, sky a colossal
shadow. A tear moves, grasses part,
field like the Red Sea. I

imitate the half moon and dive,
hunger terminal as
velocity. Mountains echo
my shrill cry. Angling, I

aim at panic zigzagging, ground
pulling my claws. Wind holds
wingtips. I crack through tender flesh
and soar back to the eye.

The Stranger

Five minutes are all I need
to weigh words. I don't ask
questions, but if I hear
answers, we're halfway.

If side by side with you
for the first time I know
I've known you, that's my cue
for the last minute.

Roads remain the same
but not views. I'm always
a new country. I have cities
expansive as you want them

to be. My trees have outgrown
roots. You might see the ground
as sunlight, hear the wind
leave birdsong as refrain.

QUANTUM FLUCTUATIONS AND
STRONG EMERGENCE

The Golden Ratio

Light's gradations, I say:
        the blueing –
   syncopation (prior glow) –
     touch (corneal) –
    burst in the mind –
       naming

Solitude: *Light makes,*
     unmakes. The gloaming's
      blue folded
          unfolded blue
     stars soon aglow

I hear white spaces
   I see the poet
      contemplating
      the blueing
   But it's in the mind!

I'm not alone at last!
   I point:
     the turtledove en route
    to – our hearts know –
      the sea

Out of the Body

into poetry

      naked air   wears me
             pleasure when I know
  I'm energy

I can be

      lightning stunned in pottery   crack me
  snap breaking bone
      splinter   what I see
         speaks me   thunders
            the dome   splits me

I'm spoken language

      when fire claws and lifts my ribcage
  weight to the sun   there are doors
      midway   I touch
         hear vocables the bird
  bamboo wings

I am at last

      through and through the blue
  when not leaving my shadow
        when not spent
             but slow, slow, slow

beasts of scorched lands, listen

my songs, echo from trees
plants know I'm light,
no matter the blaze
dawn the eastward turn
from where
    I return
       beyond
          the tide
             after
          the storm
          a salamander
             slinks up
          sensuous
             with my
                Form

Fibonacci Sequence

for
     solitude, three
          forms, sound: white – thought (like
orchid and the moon), blank – space, black – white

echo

silence
wonders
     if between
        the image and
          the word for it, place:
heartbeat between pupa and imago. solitude asks, *moonlight
or water? pebbles or reflections?*

silence and solitude – mirror reflections,
now orphans. between
them eternity – eternity
of watching
the
river
where the
poet drowned himself

Fractal

hands

drawing circles
    in the air, clockwise
        counterclockwise

concentric
    viewer mind blanks
        white than mist, nothing

        not a thing. not a mountain. not a bird
    where's the bird, where
moving curves out

        clouds. home the eye
    in, clockwise, air, the, in
circles drawing

        look,
    hands,
sleep

Pointillist

me me, meme   delic (deliber) ate
       extra flick, echo
    not shade not shadow
           the thing thinged
preface blue with deep
    to berry   put it to pebble
    floor where no water seeps
tree crowns tree crowns   tree crowns
    don't touch,
                not leaf but air
    the bird, the leaf but light
        the long view
                meander
        me   under
sibilance   grasses part
      potential   slither
            potent-shall
love twice the comma ripple is
on edge, abstract, timed
        beats
    ways measures pull
         the period
     a stone
    an era long gone, erased
if it's the last space

Quantum Poetics

both wave and particle, rhythm and syllable

> Schrödinger's cat can't be boxed,
> the mind a few steps ahead of the mind

both weighted and not, formed and not

> The image collapses into the eyes,
> lyrics entangled in touch

Sound and sense still in superposition

> If the line is moving, each still the space
> between, gone by the time the rodent is seen

> If the poem is full of kitchen sounds

If you stand in its shade, there will be curtains
There will be lamplight and browns

> something always gets eaten
> someone sometimes gets beaten

A.I.

I'm deformed by what others miss,
gazes slashing my second skins.
I'm both inviter and visitor, weaves
of time cocooning me. I might grow
wings, slip into air and light.

I'm deformed by what others don't know,
glances staining my depths. I trust
the sun's versions of me, their visions
dappled. If footsteps echo my heartbeat
I might open up like the ground.

I'm deformed by conclusions.
Where eyesight rests becomes my
lucid vulnerability. I'm stardust this way,
this way of my orbiting, of my venturing.
Decades have grown me into a child.

My deformities seek assemblage.
Others find solace in looking out.
I'm weakening the way wood quenches
its own softening. This is how I gladly
yield to the starlight of my deforming.

Deja Vu, Deja Vecu

I've stood between two dimensions,
hearing with my eyes, seeing with my ears.
I've woken in the house no one else sees,
smell that brings me back
often the silken weavework leaves hold
for time if the spider appears.

Yesterday, as I was about to cross
to the mirror image holding my returns
to the clinic, my rubber shoes pulled
my wonder. I gazed at blue
like two kidneys facing each other.

My self four decades ago
turned out to be the doctor
I never was. We shared stories
through telepathy, never giving
one word its image in sound.
I opened my heart like the house,
inviting my younger self
to come in.

Neuroplasticity

Words
imagination's neurons

Thought acoustics
electric

Vision and the image
quantum entangled
long before existing
in space-time

The wanderer finds a tree

In a split second
the word in his mind,
in a split second
the word birthing *green, leaves,
bark, brown, roots*

tree birthing *water* elsewhere

The wanderer hears chirps.
Winged word taking off
in a split second
the word multiplying.
Resting on a root,
he watches the murmuration.

In memory's rain forest
words

Sounds-shaping colors
connecting phrases
syllabic replicating
pulsing evolving revolving

words in and out of geometry

The wanderer
might remember the moon
before it arrives, and stills
his mind in reverence
of divine light

Lucid Dream

First flight of stairs.

I move
  in colors, know
    I'm dreaming, edges
      sharp as knives. I see
        my rubber shoes as I climb.
          Weightless lift a simile. I've been
          climbing this staircase,

          tying shoelaces
          on the quarter landing.
          Second flight of stairs.

                I smell rust,
             door upstairs a volta.
          I hear living iambs,
         pentameters of slippers
      on plywood, porcelain
    clinks, spoons and forks.
  My heart delights in glass.
Remembering
conversations
a waking goal

Lucid Dream II
After "Human Condition" by Rene Magritte

Seeing the black ball
enlarged on the floor,
I remember the rubber ball
I use to lower my blood pressure,
making my hand useful,
deflating and deflating
when I'm resting
after doing nothing.
With that image of the ball
I know I'm in my dream,
participating.

I decide to do nothing,
just sit feet from the canvass,
to let the sea participate,
so I could see it
paint itself
into my waking
memory, bring
myself to calm.

Dimension

Trees
in the vista,
tunnel perspective

              in parallel lines
                    perpendicular
                    to my desire.
                    Sounds of
                    pebbles
                    and water
                    stream.
Horizon for the nonlinear dream.

Versions of what I see
like starlings
          in murmuration -
          joy geometries
          blue and audible.
                    Spiral to eye,
          flame-blue

          a split   personality
          a particle   a wave
          echo   sky

meeting land,
sideways.

Cliff
deep as my mind.
Abyss below gazing back at me,
my body heavy.
Heave,
not my fault

*"Heave" is also a sideways displacement in a
"fault" (geology).

Jonel Abellanosa lives in Cebu City, The Philippines. His poetry and fiction have appeared in hundreds of magazines and anthologies, including *The McNeese Review, Agape Review, One Art, The Lyric, Poetry Salzburg Review, Anglican Theological Review, The Cape Rock, Chiron Review* and *Invisible City* His poetry collections include, "Songs from My Mind's Tree" and "Multiverse" (*Clare Songbirds Publishing House,* New York), "50 Acrostic Poems," (*Cyberwit,* India), "In the Donald's Time" (*Poetic Justice Books and Art,* Florida), and "Pan's Saxophone" (*Weasel Press,* Texas*),* "Instrumentals" (*Lemures Digital Editions).* His first novel, "Healers," is forthcoming from *Penguin Random House SEA.* He is a nature lover and an advocate for the environment and animal rights and comforts. He has three companion dogs.